nothing in LEADERSHIP STARTS until YOU START

50 Principles For Becoming An Extraordinary Leader and Achieving More Success

Mike Driggers

Copyright © 2016 IME publishing group

ALL RIGHTS RESERVED no part of this book or its associated ancillary materials may be reproduced or transmitted in any form or by any means, electronic or mechanical, including photocopying, recording, or by any information of storage or retrieval system without the permission from the publisher.

PUBLISHED BY IME Publishing Group

DISCLAIMER AND/OR LEGAL NOTICES
While all attempts have been made to verify the information provided in this book and its ancillary materials, neither the author or the publisher assume any responsibility for errors, inaccuracies or omissions and is not responsible for any financial loss by consumer in any manner. Any slights of people or organizations are unintentional. If advice concerning legal, financial, accounting or related matters is needed, the service of a qualified professional should be sought. This book and its associated axillary materials, including verbal and written training, is not intended for use as a source of legal, financial or accounting advice. You should be aware of the various laws governing business transactions or other business practices in your particular geographical location.

EARNINGS AND INCOME DISCLAIMER
With respect to the reliability, accuracy, timeliness, usefulness, adequacy, completeness, and/or suitability of information provided in the book, Mike Driggers and IME Publishing Group its Partners Associates Affiliates Consultants and/or presenters make no warranties guarantees representations or claims of any kind. Readers results will vary depending on a number of factors. Any and all claims or representations as to income earnings are not to be considered and average earnings. Testimonials are not representative. This book and all products and services are for education and informational purposes only. Use caution and see the advice of qualified professionals. Check with your accountant, attorney or professional adviser before acting on this or any information. You agreed that Mike Driggers and IME Publishing Group is not responsible for the success or failure of your personal, business, health or financial decisions relating to any information presented by Mike Driggers and IME Publishing Group or Company products/services. Earnings potentials is entirely dependent on the efforts, skills and application of the individual person.

Any examples, stories, references, or case studies are for illustrative purposes only and should not be interpreted as testimonies and/or examples of what reader and/or consumers are generally expected from the information. No representation in any part of this information, materials and/or seminar trainings are guarantees or promises for actual performance. Any statements, strategies, concepts, techniques, exercises and ideas in the information materials and/or seminar training offered are simply opinion or experience, and thus should not be misinterpreted as promises, typical results or guarantees (expressed or implied). The author and the publisher (Mike Driggers, IME Publishing Group (IME) or any IME Representatives) Shall in no way, under any circumstances be held liable to any party (or third-party) for any direct, indirect, punitive, special, incidental or other consequential damages arising directly or indirectly from any use of books, materials and or seminar trainings, which is provided "as is," and without warranties

Mike Driggers / IME Publishing Group
www.SuccessWithMikeDriggers.com
www.IMEPublishingGroup.com

IME Publishing Group/ Mike Driggers —1st ed.
ISBN: - 978-0-9973034-5-2

PRINTED IN THE UNITED STATES OF AMERICA

WHAT OTHERS ARE SAYING ABOUT MIKE DRIGGERS AND HIS STRATEGIES

Recommend To All Leaders – Great Insights!
— **Daniel Eugene** "Rudy" Ruettiger, Played football for University of Notre Dame and In 1993, TRISTAR Productions immortalized his life story with the blockbuster film, "RUDY"

Mike Driggers principles offer a fresh and timely perspective that will ignite your soul and put fuel on your internal fire to go out and be the best you can be in your personal and professional life. — **Jill Lublin**, CEO, PublicityCrashCourse.com, International Speaker & 4x Best selling Author

Whether you're a seasoned business leader, a recent graduate just starting your career or an entrepreneur, Mike Driggers principles and approach apply across all Industries and disciplines. Mike's attitude is inspiring and he is an outstanding mentor. — **Jonathan Atkinson**, Criminal Investigator Santa Clara County District Attorney's Office

Mike's ideologies to achieving everything you ever wanted in business and in Life gives you a step-by-step blueprint that will make you strive harder and push further than you ever have. — **Sonia Hinojo**, Air Liquid Sales and Marketing Manager

Mike's practical ways to becoming a high achiever in business and in your personal life through his simple to use principles are a must-have and I highly recommend you learn them now. — **Greg Kite**, Former NBA Player for the Boston Celtics & Executive Field Chairman for Hegemon Group International

GREAT meeting today--as usual, terrific atmosphere for connecting, and a great tactics and strategy exercise led by Mike. — **David Hirata**, Theatrical Modern Magician

I really appreciate the high quality of biz coaching my group has from Mike Driggers! — **Ellen Vaughn Simonin**, Physical Therapist and Acupuncturist

The ideas presented by Mike Driggers offer an inspiration and exciting perspective that will change the course of how you succeed in business or life. — **Steve Jones**, 10 years Law Enforcement

Whether you're an executive at a fortune 500 company or an entrepreneur Mike Driggers solutions go far beyond traditional business practices. Any organization can put this to immediate use and achieve amazing results. — **Steve Aust,** Former NBA Player for the Los Angeles Lakers, Chairman Co-Founder of Agora Advantage

Mike Driggers strategies are remarkable and insightful. He provides an easy-to-understand blueprint that makes you want to jump ahead and implement his process immediately.
 — **Belza López**, Housing Specialist for the City of Napa

Mike Driggers Concepts will become an invaluable tool in business and life for those who are on a pursuit of Excellence and Success. — **Gabriela Aguilera**, Orthodontic Treatment Coordinator

PROCRASTINATION KILLER
Special **FREE** Bonus Gift For **YOU!**

To help you stand out from the crowd
FREE BONUS RESOURCE for you at;
www.theprocrastinationkiller.com/procrastinationgift

Get your FREE Report And You'll Discover...

1. The Top 5 most common signs of chronic procrastinators (It could be YOU!)

2. The reasons why you're terribly UNPRODUCTIVE!

3. Your inner power to push through any procrastination pitfall

www.theprocrastinationkiller.com/procrastinationgift

Nothing In LEADERSHIP Starts Until YOU Start

"Share This Book"

Retail 24.95

Special Quantity Discounts

5-20 Books	21.95
21-99 Books	18.95
100-499 Books	15.95
500-999 Books	10.95
1,000 + Books	8.95

To Order Go To www.BookMikeToday.com

THE IDEAL PROFESSIONAL SPEAKER FOR YOUR NEXT EVENT!

Any organization that wants to develop and grow their business to become "extraordinary" needs to hire Mike for a keynote and or workshop training!

TO CONTACT OR BOOK MIKE TO SPEAK:

IME Publishing Group

(866) 7BOOKME

(866) 726-6563

www.BookMikeToday.com

Info@SuccessWithMikeDriggers.com

DEDICATION

*Many thanks and praises to GOD Almighty
who has guided me on the path that he has chosen for me.*

*This book is dedicated to my son Alex who is my driving spirit and
my greatest accomplishment in life.*

*My thanks go to my Mother and Father, who have always believed in
me and have encouraged me to reach for the stars.*

*A Special Thanks goes out to my sweetheart, Gaby Aguilera, who has
played a tremendous part in helping make this book a reality.
Also, great thanks to James Malinchak who helped with the
finer details of the concepts. And Special Thanks to Ed Melliza
photography.*

*Special Thanks to all the great mentors, coaches and business partners
whose teachings have had a profound impact on my personal and
business life.*

CONTENTS

A Message To You xv

Introduction xix

Principle 1. Personal Awareness: Understand Yourself by Acknowledging Your Strengths and Weaknesses 1

Principle 2. Passion: Possess the Drive to Pursue Perfection 5

Principle 3. Integrity: Be a Person of Strong Moral Principles and Honor 7

Principle 4. Decisiveness: Make Resolute Decisions to Attain Definite Results 11

Principle 5. Commitment: Foster Dedication Among Your People and Involvement in Your Work 15

Principle 6. Humility: Openly Accept Your Flaws as You Would Accept Other People's Strengths 19

Principle 7. Respect: Look at Every Person with a Sense of Significance 21

Principle 8. Professionalism: Act the Part and Observe Proper Work Ethics 25

Principle 9. Diplomacy: Understand the Basic Rules of Professional Negotiation 29

Principle 10. Self-discipline: Do What Must Be Done and Don't What Mustn't 33

Principle 11. Endurance: Have the Strength to Withstand Difficulties and the Persistence to Overcome Obstacles 35

Principle 12. Mindset of a Winner: Remove the Ceiling to Your Potential by Recognizing the Winner in You 39

Principle 13. Preparedness: Never Commit Without Being Equipped 43

Principle 14. Open-mindedness: Practice Flexibility and Openness to Change and New Ideas 47

Principle 15. Timeliness: Stay Updated with the Latest Business Trends and Group-Work Approaches 51

Principle 16. Creativity: Explore and Innovate for a More Dynamic Work-Performance 55

Principle 17. Selflessness: Learn to Put Your Team's Welfare Before Your Own Ego 57

Principle 18. Organizational Awareness: Understand Your Organization's Dynamics Inside and Out 59

Principle 19. Empathy: Put Yourself in Other People's Shoes to Understand Their Wants and Needs 63

Principle 20. Communication: Connect With Your People through Constant Exchange of Ideas and Information 67

Principle 21. Eloquence: Be Persuasive by Getting the Right Message Across with Clarity 71

Principle 22. Trust-Worthiness: Gain Trust and Build Trust Among Your People 75

Principle 23. Role Model Credibility: Aim to be a Leader and Not a Tyrant 79

Principle 24. Initiative: Be Courageous About Taking the First Step to Get Things Done 81

Principle 25. Generosity in Wisdom: Share your Knowledge and Experiences 83

Principle 26. Optimism: Be the Bearer of Positivity 87

Principle 27. Humor: Take Optimistic Leadership One Step Further 91

Principle 28. Transparency: Let People See Through Your Honesty 95

Principle 29. Focus: Direct Your Attention Where It Is Necessary 99

Principle 30. Punctuality: Learn to Value Time and Meet Your Deadlines 103

Principle 31. Discernment: Be Keen on Observing the Details 107

Principle 32. Goal-Setting: Identify Short Term and Long Term Goals 111

Principle 33. Levelheadedness: Use Logic and Rationale on Everyday Decisions 115

Principle 34. Fairness: Treat the Members of Your Work Force Justly 119

Principle 35. Inquisitiveness: Have a Critical Eye for Information 123

Principle 36. Constructiveness: Criticize to Improve and Not to Discourage 127

Principle 37. Encouraging Nature: Have a Nurturing Approach in Leadership 131

Principle 38. Consideration: Give a Chance to Those Who Deserve It 135

Principle 39. Practicality: Make the Most Out of Every Situation and Available Resources 139

Principle 40. Entrepreneurship: Have a Business-minded Point of View on Development and Sustenance 143

Principle 41. Team-Oriented Mindset: Make Team Growth a Permanent Objective 147

Principle 42. Friendliness: Put a Borderline Between Being a Leader and Being a Buddy 151

Principle 43. Delegation: Assign Tasks to the Appropriate Talents . 155

Principle 44. Balance: Integrate a Healthy Work-Life Balance 159

Principle 45. Political Awareness: Learn the Rules, Culture, and the Risks of Having Authoritative Powers 163

Principle 46. Assertiveness: Have a Go-Getter Attitude 167

Principle 47. Responsibility: Don't be afraid to Become Accountable 169

Principle 48. Problem-solving: Don't Cope With the Problem, Solve Them 171

Principle 49. Excellence: Set Standards and Exceed Them 175

Principle 50. Consistency: Keep Up the Good Work 179

One Last Message 181

Author Bio 185

> "EVERY MASTER WAS A DISASTER BEFORE THEY BECAME A MASTER OF THEIR TRADE. TEACH TO TEACH AS YOU LEAD AND YOU WILL BECOME THE MASTER"

A MESSAGE TO YOU!

Hi, I'm Mike Driggers, and I wanted to congratulate you on the wise decision to continue your education and the investment you just made in yourself..

I'm extremely proud of your decision to invest in you because you have literally done what most people will not do. I believe that this is the biggest reasons why people fail to achieve the results that they desire in their personal and professional lives.

Most people do not invest time or money into any type of continued education once they have finished schooling in order to learn new strategies that can create successful results. What's funny is that these are the same people that sit around complaining and blame society for their lack of success and it is never them. I am sure you are familiar with what I'm talking about. We all have either met or know someone who has this disease called excusitis. They us the "if it wasn't for" saying.

If it wasn't for the economy, president, location, my boss, I would have...

These are the type of people that always place blame on others issues. They would rather spend time focusing on why it can't be done than making a decision to take action and focus on why they can and what they need to do to make it happen.

However, this is why you will stand out from the rest. You are different because you have decided to take action by continuing your education and investing in yourself. Because of this I have a incredible amount of respect for you.

One of my favorite quotes that illustrates my point is

> *"I am not a product of my circumstances.
> I am a product of my decisions." — Stephen Covey.*

It is the mindset that makes a difference in your outcome. Every action has a reaction and the decision you make whether positive or negative determines the outcome. Making the decision to invest in yourself always has the highest returns. In all the courses and books I have spent money on I have never looked at it as spent money I looked at it as I have invested in me just like you have with investing in you with this book.

I look at your decision as you want to be better and you have invested in yourself to do so. I believe your success will be in direct proportion to your continues personal development. I am in celebration for your decision not because you bought my book but because are continuing to develop YOU.

Why did I put these principles together in a book

Earlier in my career, I learned from different mentors in my life and these are a collection of different principles I have developed, perfected and applied in my career. So, I decided to pay it forward. I would put them in a book, to give back and provide a tool for others like you so you can use in your future success.

In this book I have listed 50 simple, yet powerful principles that I believe will take you to a higher performance level in your business, sales, leadership and in your Life. They are all individual principles that are organized in a manner that makes each independent of the others. You can read or do not need to read in a sequential order. You could just simply flip through to any principles that appeals to you or read them in order either way works.

Some principles will be new to you while others will be a reminder. Some you will easily be able to implement. While others may take a little bit of extra effort. Some of these principles will comfort you. While others will change your old paradigm. One thing is for certain, these principles will have you thinking and acting differently. I sincerely hope we can meet in person here in the near future. However, until then it is my great honor to meet you through the pages of this book.

"LEADERSHIP IS SOMETHING THAT EMERGES WHEN ONE PERSON HAS PASSION, VISION AND A COOL LEVEL HEAD TO EXECUTE ON THEIR PLAN TO MAKE THAT VISION A REALITY."

INTRODUCTION

Do you consider yourself a great leader? Leadership skills are highly sought after by employers. Leadership is challenging. It's part science and part art. The science can be learned conventionally. The art is learned by experience. The ability to combine both separates the great leaders from the rest. The business environment is rapidly changing. This is creating a great demand for those with leadership skills, particularly as it relates to leading others through change. In the past, managers were tasked with maintaining the status quo. This is no longer true. If you can lead others through change, you possess one of the most valuable workplace skills.

Leaders have the ability to change companies and the world. Leadership skills are highly learnable and always valuable. Advancing your skills may be the best way to advance your career. The debate over whether leadership skills are innate or learned has likely been debated since the days of the cave man. Is it possible that some people are born with the gift of effective leadership skills while the rest of us are relegated to be full-time followers? Or is it possible that anyone can be a great leader?

While it's debatable whether everyone has the ability to become the next Winston Churchill or Mahatma Gandhi, there's little doubt that we are all capable of becoming effective leaders. Even a moderate increase in your leadership skills can have a positive impact on your personal and professional life.

Many experts hold fast to the belief that leaders are created. You may be surprised to know that it takes a good follower to be a great leader. Everyone has a boss – whether it's a supervisor in a factory, a CEO of a Fortune 500 company – or the President of the United States. All of us have someone that we must listen to and certain rules that we must adhere to. You can be a leader in your own sphere, but you must recognize that you have a boss and know that how you follow can make you a great leader. It's simply a matter of learning the necessary skills and gaining the necessary experience. Fortunately, there's never been a better time to enhance your leadership skills. There's a plethora of information available, and it's often free. In addition, researchers are hard at work to gain a better understanding of what makes great leaders tick. Business and psychology programs are constantly researching leadership topics.

Many of the famous leaders throughout history have learned their leadership skills on the fly by watching and learning from others. They were also passionate about a worthy cause and developed the ability to lead and inspire others along the way. They weren't all born to be historical figures. Most importantly, you can greatly improve your leadership skills, regardless of your current level of expertise. Being shy or introverted won't prevent you from becoming an effective leader. In fact, many of history's greatest leaders were introverts!

If you've always wanted to become an effective leader, you're in luck. There has never been a better time to enhance your ability to lead others. There are more opportunities to learn these skills than ever before. There's also never been a greater need for these skills. In this book you find 50 principles to becoming an extraordinary leader and achieve more success throughout your personal and professional life. You will learn how to be an effective leader and it will all start from YOU. Look them over; give some thought to each of them; and adapt the principles to your own leadership efforts.

> "GOOD LEADERS BELIEVE IN WHAT THEY'RE DOING. LEARN YOUR 'WHY' AND BE PASSIONATE, THEN LEAD."

PRINCIPLE 1

PERSONAL AWARENESS: UNDERSTAND YOURSELF BY ACKNOWLEDGING YOUR STRENGTHS AND WEAKNESSES

Nothing in leadership starts until you start. In order to bring out your best qualities as a leader, you must acknowledge all of your strengths and weaknesses without any personal bias or excuses. Your strengths include your talents, your skills, and the parts of your character or personality which you and the people around you may admire. On the other hand, your weaknesses include the relevant talents which you don't possess, the skills which you may be lacking, and the flaws in your personality which may be hindering your progress in different aspects of life.

By recognizing your strengths, you are recognizing all the positive things which you are capable of accomplishing. Meanwhile, by accepting your weaknesses, you begin to understand your flaws and the things that must be improved about yourself. Here are a few techniques that may help you enhance your personal awareness:

Take Psychometric tests: Psychometric tests will help you evaluate your personal traits, behavior, strengths, weaknesses, and self-perception more objectively. This type of evaluation is often divided into four categories: Verbal, Non-verbal, Numerical, and Logical-reasoning.

Although Psychometric tests are often given by corporations

as part of their applicant-assessment during employment, you may talk to the head of your organization's HR department, or you may approach a professional Psychologist outside of your office, to conduct a thorough evaluation of your results. Examples of Psychometric tests are the OCEAN model and the Myers-Briggs Type Indicator. The former evaluates the examinee's level of Openness, Conscientiousness, Extraversion, Agreeableness, and Neuroticism. Meanwhile, the latter evaluates which side of each trait-scale is more dominant for the examinee. The scales for Myers-Briggs are Extraversion-or-Introversion, Sensing-or-Intuition, Thinking-or-Feeling, and Judging-or-Perception.

Write on a daily journal: Writing about your experiences, thoughts, and feelings on a daily basis will help you enhance your sense of introspection. By recording your day-to-day internal and external experiences, you organize your thoughts and make assessments on what can make a positive or a negative impact on your moods, emotions, and environment.

Have a feedback-and-meditation routine: Instead of waiting for a monthly or quarterly performance-assessment at work, ask your friends and coworkers to give you feedback on a weekly basis. They may tell you face-to-face or you may give them a small notepad where they can write down their thoughts and opinions about your work performance and attitude.

At the end of the day, review their evaluations and meditate. Don't get angry or excited about the feedback which you have received. Instead, assess how much of these feedback are true. Think about how you can maintain the positive feedback, and how you can change your performance or your attitude to prevent the negative ones from coming back.

Please be reminded that it is important to carry out these techniques with honesty and enthusiasm in order to become effective. Remember that having a sincere personal awareness is a strength in itself. This is why no matter how busy you may become with your everyday life, you should always give time for introspection.

> "TRY TO THRIVE, NOT JUST SURVIVE. YOUR GOAL IS DEVELOP, GROW AND STRENGTHEN YOUR TEAM."

PRINCIPLE 2

PASSION: POSSESS THE DRIVE TO PURSUE PERFECTION

As a leader, the drive needed to accomplish tasks should start with you. This means that your inspiration and motivation tank should never be empty. Having the passion for the things you do will serve as a natural self-motivation force to accomplish tasks with enthusiasm and high-quality results. If you love your work, doing it will feel less like a serious task and more of an enjoyable and fundamental activity. If you don't already love your work, here are some tips to enhance your passion for your career and day-to-day tasks:

1. Choose a job or a project that is within the scope of your interests: If you haven't gotten yourself into a professional commitment yet, find out what are the things you are passionate about before applying for a particular job or deciding on a specific career path. Consider which professions you are most interested in before conducting a job-search so you don't end up landing in a long-term professional commitment which might dissatisfy you due to boredom or lack of enthusiasm.

2. Be willing to take risks and try out new things: This will help you discover the other things in your job-- or in your life in general, which you are passionate about. Although it is a great idea to choose projects within your scope of interests, always leave room for discovery. You'll never know what other things ahead might spark your passion. For example, if your company assigns you to a project which you might not have

any experience on handling yet, don't instantly reject it due to fear or lack of confidence. Give yourself a chance to discover the areas which may be new to your skills and expertise. Not only will this keep you alert and interested as you do your job, it will also help you go beyond your boundaries.

3. Identify what you aim to achieve in life: Extend your passion for your goals into your work. Use this as a motivational force to accomplish the tasks at hand. This way, you don't have to look further for reasons to get your work done, because accomplishing a task successfully will feel like a reward in itself.

4. Bring a dash of your hobbies and artistic skills to your work: Adding a little creative inspiration to your job will help give you a more fun and refreshing outlook when getting serious tasks done. It can be as little as decorating your work area with a few items of your favorite movie characters or hitting the karaoke bar with your co-workers during lunch breaks. Feel free to take the initiative to apply your hobbies and artistic skills into the process of accomplishing tasks as well. For example, if you have a knack for animation and graphics, add a little spice to your PowerPoint presentations. You can also offer your help in making dioramas and visual aids for your department's product samples.

Although every job has its own set of demands, remember that possessing an exceptional amount of interest for it will help you create the self-motivation needed to pursue perfection.

PRINCIPLE 3

INTEGRITY: BE A PERSON OF STRONG MORAL PRINCIPLES AND HONOR

Integrity is important in leadership as this reflects your personal character inside and outside of work among your colleagues and subordinates. Some people often mistake integrity as an outward appearance of having a clean and impressive personal background. Do not become one of these people, as putting up a facade will only corrupt your self-perception and personal growth. When you keep your integrity at a superficial level, you will not be able to see your flaws in their entirety and you will have little room to improve whatever you may lack in your attitude and skills. A superficial integrity will result to self-denial and hypocrisy because this would mean that you'll have to keep your guard up in order to pretend that you're an agreeable character. Avoid living with a superficial integrity by becoming a genuine person with strong moral principles. This way, being liked and respected as a leader will come to you more naturally.

To become a person deserving of respect and admiration from your subordinates, it is important to have wholeness of character. Only then will you be able to attain genuine integrity. Wholeness of character means having a firm set of values and principles to live by. Below are some examples on how to act with integrity at your workplace:

1. Stay courteous: Display politeness in everything you do. Never shout at a co-worker or a subordinate when

you are angry and avoid throwing tantrums when you don't get your way.

2. Observe basic office rules: Whether it's the dress code or something as simple as cleanliness protocols in your work space, make sure to follow these rules and remind others to follow them as well.

3. Live by your personal code of conduct: If somebody in the organization which you are working for asks you to do something that is against your values, firmly but politely refuse them. Should they insist or threaten you in any manner, don't be afraid to stand up for yourself. If you think that you have to quit your job, then don't hesitate to do it.

4. Never turn a blind eye to suspicious and wrong acts: If you see a person at work doing corrupted things, report them to the respective authorities immediately. Be it something as simple as cheating on performance evaluation, or something as grave as witnessing an illegal transaction among your superiors, never turn a blind eye on wrong doings. Taking the initiative to stop suspicious and illegal acts at your workplace is important because you'll never know who are the innocent people who might be put into compromise by those who are committing it. By living according to your moral values, you are protecting both yourself and the people around you from falling victim into such disagreeable incidents.

As shown in the following examples, always remember that

aside from appearing as pleasing and righteous in the eyes of the people around you, living with integrity will also help you influence them to stand up for what is right.

"A GOOD LEADER SHOULDN'T JUST BE DEALING WITH THE DAY-TO-DAY CHALLENGES OF THE BUSINESS, BUT SHOULD BE THINKING ONE STEP AHEAD."

PRINCIPLE 4

DECISIVENESS: MAKE RESOLUTE DECISIONS TO ATTAIN DEFINITE RESULTS

Being able to make resolute decisions shows the people around you that you are a decisive person. Decisiveness is an important trait for every leader as it is one of the proofs of having a clear mind and a firm personality. When you make resolute decisions, you don't leave people around you second-guessing and you are able to pass important messages precisely and efficiently. You give people a clear message containing a "yes" or a "no" and never a "maybe". Lack of certainty in your decision-making skills may result to a waste of time and effort. Meanwhile, the presence thereof will enhance the trust and confidence among your coworkers and team members. When people observe that they are talking to a decisive person, it assures them that they are listening to the right person with the right message. This is especially important when passing orders to your team members and subordinates.

However, being decisive does not mean that you have to make your decisions haphazardly. Making hasty generalizations is different from making resolute decisions. Decisiveness must be accompanied by tact and wit. Always validate the information and the circumstances that affect your decisions before officially proclaiming it to your team members. Here are some tips that will improve your decisiveness:

1. Stop second-guessing: Be systematic in considering all your available options. As much as possible, use a checklist or any type of visual aid to help you visualize your options in a systematic manner. Arrange your options in ascending manner from least applicable to most applicable. Under each option, write down any possible scenario or effect it would lead to.

2. Find the source of your doubts: If you have already ruled out your options but you still find yourself hesitant on making your final decision, analyze the possible source of your doubts. However, don't simply wallow over the possibilities inside your head. Instead, do the same checklist-system suggested in the tip above. List down all the possible reasons for your doubts and write below each item how you can overcome it.

3. Time Yourself: Consider decision-making as a drill. Every time that you have a difficult decision to make, allot a particular time during the day to ponder over it. This will prevent you from wasting time over being trapped in uncertainties. For example, if you have to make a decision at work about whether or not you should push through with a particular project, give yourself thirty minutes to an hour to think about the matter. Apply tips 1 and 2 to achieve more efficient and sensible results. This way, you would be able to make decisions at a faster and a more systematic pace.

4. Seek professional help: If you know that one of the major reasons that you can't make a definite decision is because

you don't have enough knowledge on the matter, don't hesitate to seek guidance from someone who knows about it better than you do. As a leader, you must put aside your personal ego and focus on doing what is best in order to solve the problems at hand.

> "A LEADER IS BEST WHEN PEOPLE IF THEY BELIEVE IN YOUR VISION, THEY WILL BE ABSOLUTELY LOYAL AND ABSOLUTELY COMMITTED TO WHAT YOU'RE DOING."

PRINCIPLE 5

COMMITMENT: FOSTER DEDICATION AMONG YOUR PEOPLE AND INVOLVEMENT IN YOUR WORK

According to psychologists and human-resource management experts, an employee's level of commitment affects the level of their work involvement. As a leader, you should become the embodiment of commitment among the group that you lead. When the circumstances take a challenging turn, you should be the last person to consider quitting from accomplishing the task at hand.

To become committed means to pledge to do a certain task or to give a certain thing for a particular cause with the best of your abilities. To be specific however, a book on Work Attitudes and Motivation by Pennsylvania State University World Campus (PSUWC) in 2013, states that an employee's commitment to an organization is closely related to loyalty or allegiance. Being a leader, your work commitment should not be limited to your own career path, but it should extend to your team and to the whole organization as well.

It is important to understand the different categories of organizational commitment in order to cultivate the same level of loyalty and involvement among the members of your organization. According to Slack, Orife, and Andersen on their study in 2010 about the "Effects of Commitment to Corporate Vision on Employee Satisfaction with Their Organization", there are three categories of organizational commitment:

1. Affective Commitment: This type of commitment is tied to an employee's loyalty to a company or organization. Basically, an employee's commitment roots from his or her belief in the company's strengths and abilities. This type of commitment is difficult to cultivate in employees of organizations that doesn't have a fully established reputation in its industry yet.

2. Continuance Commitment: This type of commitment is based on an employee's personal need to provide for his or her personal necessities. An employee stays with the company because the costs of leaving it might cause him or her more inconvenience than he or she would bargain for.

3. Normative Commitment: This type of commitment roots from an employee's feelings of obligation. An employee stays in a company and does his or her best out of fear of disappointing his or her employers and superiors.

Whatever kind of commitment you or your teammates have for your organization, it is important for you as the leader, to teach them how to translate it into a productive work-involvement. Remember that commitment is the backbone for a productive and efficient teamwork. When you build and sustain a sense of commitment among your people, you will be able to work through conflicts together at a more synchronized pace. You and the rest of your group will feel a sense of responsibility to support each other through the triumphs and challenges that you will face as members of the same organization.

> "IF YOU CAN INSPIRE YOUR TEAM TO WORK, THEN YOU CAN GET THE VERY BEST OUT OF THEM NO MATTER WHAT ELSE."

> "TAKE RESPONSIBILITY FOR YOUR ACTIONS. THAT MEANS THAT THE BUCK STOPS WITH YOU WHEN THINGS GO WRONG."

PRINCIPLE 6

HUMILITY: OPENLY ACCEPT YOUR FLAWS AS YOU WOULD ACCEPT OTHER PEOPLE'S STRENGTHS

A lot of people think humility is a trait synonymous to meekness and modesty. Although this may be true, one should not mistake this trait as a way of understating your self-confidence or restraining yourself from showcasing your skills and talents. You can still be proud about your own abilities and stay humble. Humility in its most basic English language definition, is the quality or state of mental understanding that you are not better than other people. This means that you have to accept the fact that there are people out there who are capable of surpassing your knowledge and abilities no matter how highly you think of yourself at this point in time.

Being a leader requires skills and talents that others may not always possess. It is also a basic truth that leaders, being holders of higher professional position than their subordinates, are entitled to give out commands and implement rules whenever the situation calls for it. Although these traits and advantages will make you feel special being a leader, this doesn't mean that the people around you are inferior to you or are any less capable of accomplishing positive things.

Being a leader shouldn't make you feel superior; it shouldn't give you the perception that you will always know better than they do. Every person in your social circle and work community comes from a different social background and has had different work and life experiences. This means that there may be things out there which may or may not be related to your field of expertise that they have more knowledge about than you do.

As a leader, you must recognize both the negative traits and the positive traits in every individual whom you will lead. This ability to recognize the strengths and flaws in everyone is one of the things that will make people want to follow you. Sincere understanding leads to trust and confidence. This applies to every kind of healthy relationship, particularly to a leader-follower one. Whenever you recognize and correct your team members' mistakes, never fail to show appreciation for their positive accomplishments as well.

Although it is important to have a headstrong image among your circle, never be afraid to admit when you need other people's help, even if they might belong to a rank different from yours. It doesn't matter if they have a higher or a lower social or professional position. If you know that their knowledge and talents will be of help in the progress of a project or a situation at hand, don't hesitate to be the first person to seek their guidance. If they see that you recognize and appreciate their talents and skills, they would feel honored to be of assistance to you. This humble practice of recognizing their skills and accepting your own weaknesses is one way of showing them that it is possible to have a harmonious relationship with you as their leader. This will open up possibilities to new partnerships and strengthen the workforce of your team.

PRINCIPLE 7

RESPECT: LOOK AT EVERY PERSON WITH A SENSE OF SIGNIFICANCE

The previous principle highlights the importance of humility in recognizing other people's strengths as you should accept your weaknesses. This next principle highlights the importance of recognizing people's significance as an entire person through respect. Respect, in its most basic definition in the English language, is the perception that something should be treated with seriousness or significance. In that sense, humility and respect come hand in hand.

Earning people's recognition as an individual is important to be recognized and obeyed as a leader. If you are only regarded by your teammates or subordinates as a leader because you hold a higher position than they do, there is a chance that they will only listen and work with you halfheartedly. Having halfhearted employees will decrease the efficiency and quality of your work outputs as an entire organization. To avoid this, you must become a person worth of their sincere respect both inside and outside of work.

In order to be regarded as a person worth of admiration and significance, you must do the same with the people around you first. This is where the saying "Respect is earned and not given", comes in. Here are a few examples on how you can gain your team members' and subordinates' respect:

1. Show appreciation: When somebody does a good job, never fail to show your appreciation for their efforts. Show that their accomplishments are significant to the whole organization no matter how big or small. It can be something as simple as patting your office janitor on the back for always maintaining the office space clean, or as big as helping one of your team mates in getting a salary raise or a promotion by writing them a letter of endorsement to your HR department.

2. Don't cross personal boundaries: Although it is important to get to know your team members to promote camaraderie within your organization, never forget that every person is entitled to their own personal space. For example, if you have a colleague who seemed to be acting depressed around the office and you noticed that their behavior is already affecting their work performance, talk to them. Remind them of their daily tasks and extend your help not just as their superior, but as a friend. However, don't force them to share personal matters with you if they are not ready to open up about it.

3. Do not discriminate: Especially if you work in an international industry, you are bound to meet people of different nationalities, cultures and preferences. Sometimes, these diversities may seem bizarre or eccentric to us if we do not come from the same country or if we don't see things the way they do. Although having a feeling of slight alienation or puzzlement is normal to every human when being exposed to

something new, you must keep your tact and approach these differences with polite regard. Don't laugh at a person's accent, mock their appearance or alienate them for their preferences. As a leader, it is your job to show them respect by making them feel welcome in your presence so that both you and them can focus on more objective matters at hand.

> "NEVER LOSE YOUR COOL. YOU ARE THE BAROMETER FOR THE MOOD OF YOUR TEAM."

PRINCIPLE 8

PROFESSIONALISM: ACT THE PART AND OBSERVE PROPER WORK ETHICS

Professionalism is a set of traits or qualities that an individual must observe in accordance to his or her own profession. This means that you, as a working individual, must apply proper etiquette and comply with all the requirements expected from someone of your position in an organization. As a leader, this shows the people around you how serious you are about doing your job. It is a way of exercising your respect for yourself and for your own profession. When people notice that you have a high level of professionalism, they are able to see through your self-confidence at work. This strengthens their view on your credibility as a leader.

Professionalism helps individuals to draw the line between work and personal life. By focusing on the required behavior and performance, individuals are able to increase their dedication and efficiency to the tasks at hand. Note that practicing the qualities of professionalism in your work life entails observing small and simple environmental details, to something internal, such as setting your own set of principles or moral code. Below are a few basic steps on how you can show professionalism at your work place:

1. Observe proper office decorum: Follow office rules at all times. Read the office memo, the wall-signs, and if it is available, read the office handbook. Never assume

the basic office rules, especially if you are new to a particular office environment. If you are uncertain about certain rules, approach a senior workmate or ask the HR department to inform you about it. If a certain sign in a room says, "No smoking" or "Observe silence", then do as it says. If your office space has a waste segregation system, then dispose your trash in the proper bin. Consider office rules as something similar to community laws and regulations. No one should ever be above it, and anyone who fails to observe it must receive appropriate warnings and penalties regardless of their hierarchy in the organization.

2. Follow the dress code: Whether or not your workplace has a specific dress code, you must dress appropriately for your profession at all times. Mind the length, the style and colors of your attire whenever you are at work. If you are working in a corporate environment, it is best to wear clothes with solid colors that don't show too much skin. Avoid wearing open footwear and keep your hair in a neat-looking style. If you work in an active or outdoor environment, observe proper safety gears and wear comfortable clothing that will make it easier for your to move around.

3. Keep personal emotions in check: Practice control over your emotional quotient by separating your feelings about work matters from your personal issues. No matter how stressful and challenging your professional or personal circumstances are, avoid making the mistake of taking out your emotions in the most inappropriate

of scenarios. If something emotional bothers you in the middle of your work hours, take a short break and talk to a friend or approach the office Psychologist or counselor (if counseling services are available at your HR department).

4. Deliver the required output: Avoid procrastination and focus on getting the job done. The tips above will help you look like a professional, but your legitimacy as one will highly depend on the quality of your work performance and final outputs.

"Make every effort to strengthen your ability to be a master communicater"

PRINCIPLE 9

DIPLOMACY: UNDERSTAND THE BASIC RULES OF PROFESSIONAL NEGOTIATION

As a leader, it is your job to lead the negotiations and solve conflicts while maintaining the harmonious relationship among your people with those who may be involved in it. This is why you must equip yourself with the knowledge on basic diplomatic relations before you take on the responsibility of representing a group of people. Keeping a diplomatic relationship with another person or organization is one way of engaging in a professional partnership. Both parties converse about their different opinions on a matter or a conflict in order to reach a resolution that will be most agreeable to both of them. In order to do this, both parties must observe the art of proper diplomacy. Below are simple tips on how to practice diplomacy:

1. Remember to have a conversation and not a confrontation: Before you attend the appointment with the other party, remind yourself that the objective of your meeting is to negotiate. Give the other party a chance to express their points before you negate their suggestions or opinions. Likewise, do not sound too forceful when expressing your statements. If neither parties are willing to give in to the other's requests or conditions, consider making a compromise. Always leave room for the possibilities of adjusting the terms and conditions during the discussion to have a harmonious and successful negotiation.

2. Watch your manner of speaking: Never raise your voice whenever you are trying to emphasize a point. No matter how heated a discussion may become, watch your choice of words and never use foul terminologies to insult the other party. Resorting to a display of unrefined behavior will reflect your lack of emotional control and tact to logically handle arguments.

3. Back up your arguments with facts: Support your point with facts in order to emphasize its importance. If you are dealing with financial matters, consider presenting proofs consisting of graphs and previously published figures from reliable sources. If your negotiations concern planning proposals of any form, don't hesitate to bring visual aids such as maps, diagrams, or powerpoint presentations so you can use it to expound on your points and ideas.

4. Give the other party something to think about: Some people are harder to persuade than others because they tend to block off what the other person is saying in order for them to get their way. If you happen to encounter this kind of person during an important negotiation, do not be intimidated nor irritated by their behavior. Instead of expressing your ideas in the form of statements, try expressing them in the form of questions. By asking them questions, you are showing them that their opinions on your suggestions are important. This way, you are raising your chances of hooking their attention into a two-way conversation and they are more likely to take your proposal into consideration.

"EVERY PERSON LISTENS TO ONE RADIO STATION CALLED WIIFM (WHAT'S IN IT FOR ME). LEARN TO TUNE INTO THEIR STATION AND PLAY THEIR SONG AND THEY WILL FOLLOW YOU WHEN YOU LEAD"

"Never Point The Finger And Dole Out Blame. Doing This Is A Fast Way To Make Your Team Resent You And It Can Also Create In-Fighting."

PRINCIPLE 10

SELF-DISCIPLINE: DO WHAT MUST BE DONE AND DON'T WHAT MUSTN'T

As a leader, you will be in charge of keeping your people's work character well-rounded. This includes observing and practicing discipline in the workplace to enhance every team member's sense of professionalism. This is crucial to achieving consistent and efficient work performance. However, before you are able to administer the proper ways of disciplining people in groups, you have to understand first the obligations it entails at an individual level. The best way to do this is by starting with administering the trait into your own character.

Self-discipline is a self-cultivated ability to regulate your wants, needs and impulses in order to accomplish tasks as diligently as possible. When a leader has a high level of self-discipline, he is able to set a firm example to his people of what it is like to be focused and efficient. Below are simple tips to enhance self-discipline:

1. Live a healthy lifestyle: To get started, all you have to do is to keep a balanced diet, set a weekly time for light jogs, and observe proper hours for rest and leisure activities. Observing a healthy lifestyle will help you enhance your self-discipline by giving you a personal task of observing your own health. This means that you will have to monitor the amount of junk food you consume

and avoid any form of vice which may be detrimental to your health.

2. Stay away from distractions and temptations: Keep away from anything that will put your concentration into compromise. As much as possible, stay away from noisy places and distracting environments. If you are working alone, keep away from little distractions and temptations such as online-surfing and long sessions of chatting with friends. If you are sharing your work area with other people, remind them of proper office decorum to avoid rowdy behavior in the office.

3. Don't give in to self-excuses and self-justifications: Sometimes, we make justifications in order to excuse ourselves from the failure to execute a certain task or to meet the required quality of a certain output. Avoid giving in to self-justifications by reminding yourself that no type of excuse will lead to progress. Excuses are empty words that pave way to uncontrollable procrastination.

4. Have the dedication to complete your tasks: Finish everything that you start no matter how big or small of a task it may be. It can be something as little as a promise to yourself to clean up your office desk, or something more serious like a commitment to finish a business project with your peers. Do not stop until you complete a task or a commitment. Producing solid results is the best way to prove that you have a genuine amount of self-discipline.

PRINCIPLE 11

ENDURANCE: HAVE THE STRENGTH TO WITHSTAND DIFFICULTIES AND THE PERSISTENCE TO OVERCOME OBSTACLES

Endurance is not limited to physical strength. As a leader, you must have the capacity to remain mentally, psychologically and emotionally strong whenever you find yourself in the middle of stressful scenarios. A leader should be able to resist giving up when things are working against their favor. Instead of seeing these difficulties as obstacles, you should perceive them as challenges. Although you might feel a certain level of worry and stress, consider these challenges as a chance to improve your leadership skills and your team's work performance. Below are simple tips to enhance your mental, psychological, and emotional endurance:

1. Engage in brain-games during your breaks: Instead of wasting your break time browsing through random images of your favorite things online, play games that improve mental calisthenics. Choose online games that improve memory retention or mental organization such as image-flash games, Sudoku, and Tetris.

2. Avoid idle moments: According to Psychological studies, people tend to over-think and fall into depression when they are not occupied by objective matters for long periods of time. When you find yourself bored from doing repetitive tasks, don't drop it and resort to

idleness for relaxation. Instead, find something else to do in order to keep both your mind and body active. It can be as simple as taking a short walk or finding time to do some arts and crafts. Keeping your body active promotes the circulation of oxygen into your brain and it keeps your alertness level higher.

3. Get enough rest: Lack of sleep impairs your alertness and concentration. This will result to poor decision-making and slow learning pace when you are in the middle of work. It can also put you into danger because poor alertness results to slow reaction time. This leads to higher risks of fatal accidents and work blunders. A physiological effect of lack of sleep also results to a slow metabolism and low levels of happy hormones. This will make your prone to digestive problems as well as make you feel irritable throughout the day. Avoid these problems by making sure that you get the right amount of sleep. According to National Sleep Foundation, the recommended amount of sleep for adults is between seven to nine hours. If you find yourself tired or sleepy at your workplace, consider taking fifteen minutes to snooze during your breaks instead of dosing up on caffeinated or sugary drinks.

4. Take control of your emotions: Increase your emotional quotient by finding out the source of your stress and depression. Knowing what triggers your emotions will help you cope up with difficult situations through proper stress-and-anger management. When you are aware of which direction your moods are taking you,

you can prevent negative emotions from surfacing and destroying your focus. Find ways to combat unpleasant feelings though rational thinking and meditative skills.

"DEVELOP A VISION AND SHARE IT WITH YOUR TEAM. ALWAYS DEMONSTRATE YOUR VALUES. PAINT THE BIG PICTURE"

PRINCIPLE 12

MINDSET OF A WINNER: REMOVE THE CEILING TO YOUR POTENTIAL BY RECOGNIZING THE WINNER IN YOU

In order to lead a team to success, a leader must develop a winner's mindset. To have a winner's mindset means to be open about your endless potential of achieving something through effort and perseverance which is worth of positive recognition. By having a winner's mindset, you are conditioning yourself into thinking and into believing constantly that anything is possible with the right amount of dedication and application of your abilities. Having this kind of mindset will enhance your mental and psychological endurance, as well as your commitment to the tasks at hand.

Below are simple tips that will help you to develop a winner's mindset:

1. Have an endless hunger for learning: A winner is confident in his or her own skills and abilities but always leaves room for growth. You have to believe that mastery of skills isn't the final stage for self-improvement. Once you feel that you have already mastered a certain skill, expand your knowledge and your experiences by learning new things that may enhance your craft or expertise. For example, if you are currently in a managerial position at work and you have already attained a bachelor's and a master's degree related to that field, consider attending managerial workshops or seminars during your free

time to further expand your knowledge. Continue to read educational books, stay updated with the relevant events in the society, and learn from other people who have more experience than you do.

2. Never assume: Don't quickly jump into conclusions when you are analyzing a situation. Never assume that you know how things will turn out, regardless of the positivity or negativity of your predictions. When you assume things, you put a limit to your level of preparedness and to your ability to understand different situations. Always leave room for possibilities of sudden changes. Learn to adjust your strategies according to the necessities being called for by the circumstances.

3. Be persistent: One of the most typical behaviors a winner sports in the face of a challenge is persistence. Whatever type of competition he may be in, a winner never fails to get up every time he gets knocked down by an opponent or by his own weaknesses. Just like having the continuous interest for learning, you must also put a continuous effort in achieving your goals regardless of the difficulties which you might have to deal with along the way. One way of enhancing your persistence is by exercising sportsmanship. Accept your failures graciously by admitting your mistakes and by recognizing the efforts of those who were able to do better than you. Consider every failure you have made as trials and not as final results. Never stop putting interest and effort on a goal until you have achieved your desired outcome.

"EVERY MASTER WAS A DISASTER BEFORE THEY BECAME A MASTER OF THEIR TRADE. TEACH TO TEACH AS YOU LEAD AND YOU WILL BECOME THE MASTER"

"Leaders don't expect to receive more commitment than they're willing to give. Demonstrate how much you care about being successful and how they play a key role in making that happen"

PRINCIPLE 13

PREPAREDNESS: NEVER COMMIT WITHOUT BEING EQUIPPED

Leadership is a commitment that requires dedication and preparedness at all times. Similar to going to any type of battle or adventure, a leader's state of readiness should extend to all aspects of his personality. This means that before you commit into the role of being a leader, you must be equipped physically, mentally, psychologically and experientially. Below are tips to enhance your state of readiness inside and outside of your workplace:

1. Never commit without fully understanding: Don't accept responsibilities which you do not fully understand. Before accepting a task or a job, understand its rules and the right approaches to get it done. Likewise, don't be hasty when trying to solve a problem. Study the possible effects of every solution you have in mind before resorting to action.

2. Bring the right tools: Whether it's a meeting, a team-building session, or a regular day at work, always bring the right tools and equipment with you. If you are presenting something during an organization meeting, bring both soft and hard copies of your presentation for distribution among the attendees. If you are part of the audience, always take note of any important detail that will be discussed to help you come up with substantial suggestions. During team-building sessions, learn about

the new faces who might need your guidance, and the seniors you can turn to when you need assistance. When at work, always keep a back-up USB Flash or blank disc for data storage to avoid losing important documents. Most of all, stay updated on the current events within your organization. Know about the current issues and project developments your company is involved in. Use this information to formulate objectives that will help you contribute to the organization's progress.

3. Anticipate worst-case scenarios: Although staying optimistic will help in boosting your team's morale and yours, acknowledging the possibilities of situations going wrong will help you deal with unforeseen challenges better. You are less likely to get stressed out when facing an unfavorable turn of circumstance because it'll be easier for you to work out the alternative routes to cope with it. Worst-case scenarios include internal conflicts in your organization, external threats to your objectives, and environmental calamities. No matter how unlikely are the occurrence of these disasters, never underestimate the ratio of its probability. Stay informed about appropriate safety measures in case of earthquakes, floods, fire, and criminal break-ins.

4. Arrive earlier than the scheduled time: Arriving on time and meeting deadlines on the designated date are two of the best ways to prove your sense of punctuality. Take your responsibilities as a leader one step further by arriving earlier than the expected time and by accomplishing tasks before the due date. Arrive fifteen

to thirty minutes before an appointment to make extra preparations for yourself both mentally and physically. Take this time to review your objectives and to check the presentability of your appearance. Similarly, it is best to complete a project before its deadline to give yourself more time to inspect and further improve its quality before its submission.

> "ALWAYS FIND
> THE OPTIMAL WAY
> TO MOTIVATE EACH TEAM
> MEMBER"

PRINCIPLE 14

OPEN-MINDEDNESS: PRACTICE FLEXIBILITY AND OPENNESS TO CHANGE AND NEW IDEAS

Keeping an open mind will help you become more responsive to changes. This will boost your ability to comply more efficiently to your job's demands. When you are able to adjust your work-pace and way-of-thinking according to the needs of the situation, you are able to improve both your emotional control and logical abilities. This is because being flexible in handling situations allows your mind to explore different aspects of solving challenges. In turn, your instincts react to unfamiliar things with a sense of anticipation instead of apprehension. With the capacity to become flexible in handling situations, you are able to think with more clarity and less anxiety. Thus, open-mindedness is more than just a personality trait: It is a fundamental drill that requires constant practice through mental-conditioning and actual application. Below are simple tips on how to enhance open-mindedness:

1. Give old and new ideas a chance: When looking up references and ideas for developing projects or solving conflicts, consider the possibilities of utilizing both old-fashioned and modern ideas. Never disregard the learning materials you may acquire from the past, and the modern ideas that may be worth exploring in the future.

2. Don't get carried away by rumors: Never believe a

statement without significant proof. It doesn't matter if the subject of the rumor is you or someone else. Always validate the source of the rumor first and evaluate for yourself whether or not it is true. However, choose wisely which among these rumors you should give time and effort for confirmation. Don't waste your time on matters that will not bring any development to your objectives. If its confirmation will not benefit your career or help with the progress of a task at hand, it is best that you abandon any ideas of investigating it.

3. Assess the positive and the negative sides of every person and situation: Not all circumstances that may seem negative will lead to doom. Likewise, not all seemingly positive news will bring favorable results to everyone it involves. Before canceling out a negative-sounding idea, consider all the positive changes it might bring to the circumstances. Similarly, before you accept positive-sounding proposals, consider if its execution could cause any inconvenience to certain parties in may involves.

4. Show courage: When you have an open mind, some people will criticize you for not having the same conservative views as they do. Some people might even mistake your openness for lack of principles. What these people do not understand is that open-mindedness is integral for a diverse leadership. Do not be discouraged if you don't earn the support of these critics, especially if they don't even play any significant role in the achievement of your team's goal. Remember that your open-mindedness pertains to exploring new ideas and

to your adaptability to changes. It does not involve listening to naysayers who are incapable of giving you productive criticisms.

"THERE ARE MANY WAYS TO ALWAYS STRENGTHEN YOUR LEADERSHIP SKILLS. TAKE ADVANTAGE OF EVERY LEADERSHIP OPPORTUNITY TO HONE YOUR SKILLS"

PRINCIPLE 15

TIMELINESS: STAY UPDATED WITH THE LATEST BUSINESS TRENDS AND GROUP-WORK APPROACHES

This principle on timeliness is closely related to the previous principle discussed in this book. You cannot be open-minded without being aware of the current status of your social environment. Likewise, you cannot improve the present situation using new information without having the amount of adaptability only found in people who have open minds.

As a leader, you must continue to find new ways to develop your problem-solving skills and your ability to enhance your team's work performance. This will help you to continuously develop each and every member's talents and skills. Below are some tips to stay updated with the latest business trends and group-work approaches:

1. Read the newspaper: Despite seeming like an old-fashioned reading material to younger generations, using the newspaper as reference for social, political, and economic updates is still the most convenient way to attain credible and complete information. It doesn't even have to be the paper format. Checking your social media for updates on these matters may help you to stay updated on a minute-per-minute basis. However, know that most of the time, the information that spreads online is either too raw (due to real-time publishing from

unnamed sources) or had already been tainted by biased opinions from the netizens. If you are reading digital materials, such as e-zines and virtual news catalogs, make sure to only subscribe to reliable online publishers. If your community's trusted newspaper has its own website, consider keeping a link or an app to their online news portal in your gadgets so you can stay updated on a 24/7 basis.

2. Attend Seminars: Attending seminars is one of the quickest ways to get a crash course on the latest developments on your field of concern or expertise. This is more convenient than stocking up on new learning materials which you might not have the time to study due to your hectic schedule. By attending seminars, you are able to have credible speakers and coaches summarize many of the information in your areas of concern without you browsing through thick pages of texts. The open-forum sessions which take place after each talk or lecture session is also a great opportunity for you to get your questions answered by professionals right on the spot.

3. Work with talents from different generations: Every person from each generation have their own experiences and trends. Take time to get to know your team members from different age brackets. Listen to stories about their previous work experiences and conduct evaluations on what are their most preferred approaches in group work and in individual-learning.

4. Perceive technology and social media as tools: Learn to utilize technology and social media to enhance work-performance. Instead of preventing your co-workers or your teammates from getting distracted by their gadgets, use their technological attachment as an opportunity to get their attention. Consider making online group accounts and group pages to keep your team members updated on your organization's latest issues and events. Also, don't forget to stay updated on the different business software available in the market. Consider proposing to your organization to allocate a budget for the ones which you know could benefit everybody's work-performance.

> "YOUR BEHAVIOR SETS THE BOUNDARIES FOR EVERYONE ELSE"

PRINCIPLE 16

CREATIVITY: EXPLORE AND INNOVATE FOR A MORE DYNAMIC WORK-PERFORMANCE

Creativity is the ability to create new things and think of new ideas. As a leader, being creative in everything you do is important to keep your people interested in accomplishing the tasks at hand. Creativity paves way to exploration and innovation. This helps in keeping your team motivated by encouraging them to feel excited and enthusiastic about the changes that occur in their day to day work-experiences. Creativity allows you to look at things with a fresh perspective. It will help you add an interesting twist to the most mundane tasks and routines at work.

Although some individuals are born displaying higher level of creativity than most people, this ability can actually be developed by anyone with continuous practice. Below are some tips to enhance your level of creativity:

1. Trigger creativity through visual aids: Make creative-thinking a norm in your work life by using visual aids to trigger it. This can be done through something as simple as allowing yourself and your subordinates to decorate their work space. You may also consider using graphics in your visual presentations during board meetings to capture your audience's attention. One more option you should try is the application of color psychology to your work environment. According to visual artists

and psychologists, each color has a different effect on a person's emotions. Try adding vibrant colors to your workplace to lift your co-workers moods. Use colorful memo pads when tacking notes on the group tack-board, encourage owning colorful office supplies, and use pens with bright-yet-visible ink when writing down notes.

2. Explore your hobbies: Creativity can be developed though many ways aside from visual triggers. Some people may not be as good in applying visual innovations to their work outputs compared to their peers. However, this does not mean that they are less creative than the others. Explore your other creative talents by allocating time for your hobbies. Pay attention to the kind of skills and talents which you apply to your hobbies. Explore how you can apply this to your job in order to enhance your work-performance.

3. Encourage a sense of adventure: As you do your own creative exploration, try to encourage your team members to do the same. This will help your team to work together with a bolder view on the challenges ahead of them. Arrange for team-building activities that can enhance each and every member's creative ability. Include games and drills that may enhance their observation skills and sense of adventure. Investigative games are ideal for this type of team-building activity, as it encourages the players' ability to associate facts, make objective assumptions, and discover new ways of gathering evidences to solve mysteries.

PRINCIPLE 17

SELFLESSNESS: LEARN TO PUT YOUR TEAM'S WELFARE BEFORE YOUR OWN EGO

Selflessness is the practice of putting other people's welfare before your own. However, it must not be mistaken as an act of having zero regard for one's personal worth. An effective leader must understand their own strengths and weaknesses. By having personal awareness, you are able to acknowledge the skills and talents which you can use to help others. To put it simply, a leader must use his abilities to improve the welfare of his people instead of using it for his own vanities. Therefore, one must not confuse selflessness with irrational martyrdom.

Selfless leadership is effective because it allows the leader to dedicate his efforts to the development of every person in his team. This strengthens a person's trust for himself, for his peers, and for his leader. Below are tips on how to exercise selfless leadership:

1. Don't be arrogant: Being a leader gives you the advantage to pass down commands. However, holding a higher position within an organization should not equate to lack of self-involvement. As a leader, you must remind yourself that "you are working with the team" and that the team does not work for you. Be confident about your self-worth and understand that working alongside your people will not lower their respect for you. In fact, your hands-on leadership approach will more likely gain you

admiration from your subordinates and superiors alike.

2. Make team-progress part of your objectives: When you aim for excellence-- be it in your own career or in your final work-output, always include team-progress as part of your objectives. This will help you have a group-oriented approach when dealing with your job. Through this, you are maximizing your people's talents and enhancing their work-involvement.

3. Share your knowledge: Have the patience and the enthusiasm to teach your people how to accomplish tasks more effectively. Guide them by passing down your knowledge and skills. Do not worry about the possibilities of your subordinates outshining you. Rather, you should be proud that you were able to contribute to their progress. Consider passing down your wisdom as a means of leaving a legacy to your organization and to the younger generation.

4. Share the recognition: Never forget to share the credit with your group whenever you are being recognized for a job well done. If you have the chance, it would be better if you also give recognition to your members individually. This will help in the cultivation of a healthy competition among your team. It will also boost your team's morale because they know that their hard work will be given importance by their leader and by their organization. This way, you are able to help them recognize their self-worth.

PRINCIPLE 18

ORGANIZATIONAL AWARENESS: UNDERSTAND YOUR ORGANIZATION'S DYNAMICS INSIDE AND OUT

Organizational awareness helps an individual broaden his perspectives about the organization and the society he is a part of. As a leader, this helps you to address the needs of your team, as well as the needs of the entire organization more efficiently. Like all the previews principles mentioned in this e-book, organizational awareness is an ability that you must cultivate within yourself until it becomes a part of your natural leadership mindset. A few of the traits you'll need in order to put organizational awareness into practice are: Curiosity, open-mindedness, professionalism and punctuality. Below are simple ways to enhance your organizational awareness:

1. Understand the organizational structure: Learn about the hierarchy of officers and the division of departments within your organization. Get to know the names of every personnel in charge of each division and establish a professional relationship with them. Being able to keep your communications open with more people will help you understand the concerns of your organization in a more detailed manner. This is particularly important for leaders who are managing a team or a project at a micro-managerial scale because it helps them troubleshoot concerns more specifically.

2. Learn about the company's role: Learn about the kind of industry and society your organization belongs to. Understand the organization's vision and mission, and assess how you can incorporate it to your team's objectives. This will help you come up with strategic plans that are in sync with the organization's long term and short term goals. This way, you raise the significance and effectiveness of your work performance and overall outputs.

3. Pay attention to the organization's issues: Stay up-to-date on the economic, political, and social issues that may bring impact to the organization's operations and overall standing in the industry. Being aware of the circumstances surrounding your organization will help you to determine which external threats and opportunities you should pay close attention to. Expanding your views outside of the organization's internal environment will particularly help in studying the extent of your managerial strategies' effectiveness.

4. Encourage social awareness among your people: Encouraging the members of your organization to stay updated on the overall issues that surround the society and the environment enhances their concern for non-personal affairs. By raising social awareness among your people, you cultivate their ability to internalize on how daily external circumstances affect their lives. This will make it easier for you to make them realize the importance of being aware of the structure and the dynamics of the organization which they are a

part of. As a result, you cultivate their sense of work-involvement. Your team members are more likely to realize the significance of accomplishing a task when they know the kind of impact their efforts can bring to the organization.

> "BE LIKABLE, BUT SERIOUS. IF YOU'RE LIKABLE, OTHERS WILL DO THEIR BEST TO HELP YOU"

PRINCIPLE 19

EMPATHY: PUT YOURSELF IN OTHER PEOPLE'S SHOES TO UNDERSTAND THEIR WANTS AND NEEDS

An effective leader should possess the ability to persuade different types of people. Despite the boundaries of professionalism that must be observed, a leader must know how to relate with his people at a personal level in order to keep a harmonious and productive relationship with them. Understand their wants and need to find work-approaches that will keep them motivated and interested for longer periods of time. Particularly, you will be able to enhance your approach on team-dynamism, rewards-system, and diplomatic negotiations. Below are tips on how to enhance your social empathy:

1. Learn to read between the lines: Communication skills may vary among the people within your organization. As a leader, you should pay close attention to the way a person delivers his or her message to assure that you understand their point with precision. Pay particular attention to their body language, conversational tone, and facial expressions. If a person acts too stiff or too anxious during a conversation, there is a high possibility that they are not giving you all the information necessary for you to obtain a clear conclusion. It will help you to clarify their points by briefly re-stating it before you proceed with giving your own input on the matter at hand.

2. For example, if you have a new intern at work and he seems anxious about passing down a command from another department to you, try responding to him in this manner: "The head of the HR department wants me to be present in their appointment tomorrow, correct? Thank you for relaying his message. Please let him know that I will certainly attend tomorrow's meeting."-- By re-stating their message, you are able to ask for clarification and still express how closely you are paying attention to them.

3. Watch your body language: Just as how you must observe other people's body language, so should you do the same to yours. Having a strict reputation as a leader might intimidate some people and make them hesitant about approaching you. Keep your conversational stance accommodating by keeping your facial expression neutral and your posture more relaxed, without looking too lazy or uninterested. By giving a more open impression towards your team, you are inviting them to relate and express their concerns with you better.

4. Encourage peer-interaction: Although chatting-time is often discouraged among workers during their work-hours, it may be the way to enhance team camaraderie. Allot time and specific activities for your team members to have productive conversations with each other. Let them talk about their hobbies, family, work-concerns and motivations openly on specific occasions. This will raise their empathy for each other and build trust for a more efficient team work.

> "THE MOST IMPORTANT PART OF CREATING A WORKING TEAM IS TO UNDERSTAND THE DIFFERENT CHARACTERS AND WHAT THEY CAN EACH BRING TO YOUR ORGANIZATION."

> "UNDERSTANDING THE CAPABILITIES OF EVERYONE ON YOUR TEAM HELPS YOU TO ASSIGN TASKS TO EACH MEMBER THAT ARE APPROPRIATE TO THEIR SKILLS"

PRINCIPLE 20

COMMUNICATION: CONNECT WITH YOUR PEOPLE THROUGH CONSTANT EXCHANGE OF IDEAS AND INFORMATION

Some people confuse communication with talking in front of another person. Note that orally communicating with others is a mode of communication: It does not define communication itself. Communication is the act of exchanging messages with one another. These messages may be ideas, opinions, or information which are transferred from the sender to the receiver through oral, written, or visual means. As a leader, you must be able to promote effective circulation of ideas and information to keep the unity among your people. This in turn, will promote the synchronization of work-performance.

This principle is most effective when applied hand-in-hand with the other principles mentioned in this e-book. To be able to communicate effectively, you must be respectful, professional, diplomatic, and empathetic. Below are tips for effective communication:

1. Choose appropriate conversation scenarios: Choose the appropriate time and place to have a conversation. Whether it's a web conference, a phone conversation, or an actual face-to-face conversation, always consider the atmosphere and the amount of noise in the background. Make sure that you are in a venue where you and the people involved in the conversation will hear and

understand each other.

2. Don't resort to blaming: When conflicts arise in the middle of your communication process, avoid pointing fingers at anybody. Don't focus your emotions on the other party. Instead, focus on how to solve the issue at hand which has become the root of your conflict and negative emotions.

3. Listen with interest: To sit down and to hear what a person has to say is different from actually listening to them. When you listen to a person, you ponder about the ideas, the opinions and the information that they share with you. An effective communication flow should have a message-sender who can connect with a message-receiver with clarity. In return, a message-receiver must be able to give the message-sender an appropriate feedback. Become an interactive listener by sharing your thoughts and opinions concerning the matters that are being discussed during the communication process be it oral or written.

4. Explain your ideas: Whether it is a written or an oral conversation, you must always make your statements clear. Don't assume that people will understand your decisions and the meaning behind your actions. Organize the flow of your thoughts before sharing your message to its respective recipients.

5. Draw the line between facts and opinions: Don't use your authority as a leader to state your opinions as facts. This will make people feel that you are forcing your

opinions on them without considering their inputs. Draw the line between facts and opinions by clearly defining which one you are expressing: When stating opinions, start your sentences with "I think", "Perhaps", "In my opinion", or "Based on my observation". Whenever you are stating facts, don't forget to cite or mention your sources.

"IN COMMUNICATION SPEAKING MORE SLOWLY MAKES YOU SEEM CALMER, MORE CONFIDENT AND MORE INTELLIGENT!"

PRINCIPLE 21

ELOQUENCE: BE PERSUASIVE BY GETTING THE RIGHT MESSAGE ACROSS WITH CLARITY

Eloquence is the skill of speaking or writing with fluency which results to powerful persuasion. This is different from person-to-person communication as the effectiveness of the message-delivery relies on the sender. The speaker or the writer must be able to get his or her message across to his audience without expecting any impromptu verbal feedback. A common action that requires eloquence is public-speaking.

As a leader, there will be a lot of instances when you must convey your message to a whole group of people instead of doing it from person to person. There will be moments when you'll be required to pass down instructions, words of encouragement, and memo announcements orally to your whole team in order to save time and energy. This usually happens when you are caught in a hectic schedule or when you are rushing to finish an output that requires synchronized team work. Below are tips to enhance your eloquence:

1. Know your audience: As an eloquent speaker, you must be able to establish an emotional and a logical connection with your audience. Learn to adjust your language and your manner of speaking according to your audience's level of understanding and communication norms. Consider the age, the culture, the profession, and the personality of your audience. This will help you determine

their attention span, commonly used expressions, and extent of verbal and technical understanding. It is also important for you to know which issues concern them and which ones offend them. Show empathy for the former and avoid brushing on the topics related to the latter. This way, you are more likely to keep your audience in a positive mood throughout your speech.

2. Make your content substantial: The substance of your content is determined by its significance to the issue at hand. Although it is important to avoid sounding emotionless when delivering your message, avoid going around in circles when you are trying to emphasize your points. Make sure that your speech or your letter addresses the concerns of your audience and that it is told straight to the point. Organize your content's flow of thought and keep the whole composition precise and concise.

3. Keep your delivery natural: When you deliver a speech, your posture, intonation, and organization of ideas are observed by your audience. Show them that you are confident in yourself and in your topic by being physically and mentally prepared. Dress appropriately and keep your posture upright and yet natural. Keep a firm expression on your face and maintain eye-contact with your audience but avoid looking too stiff. To prevent getting lost in your topic, prepare cue cards that contain the subject-flow of your speech. If you're expressing your message through written content, keep your tone formal but pleasant.

"IN COMMUNICATION SPEAKING MORE SLOWLY MAKES YOU SEEM CALMER, MORE CONFIDENT AND MORE INTELLIGENT!"

> "LEADERS ARE HONEST. ALL RELATIONSHIPS REQUIRE A FOUNDATION OF TRUST TO ENSURE SUCCESS"

PRINCIPLE 22

TRUST-WORTHINESS: GAIN TRUST AND BUILD TRUST AMONG YOUR PEOPLE

Gaining the trust of your people will increase their respect for you as a leader and as an individual. Building a reputation of being a trust-worthy person will make it easier for your people to report to you the arising issues in your organization or your work place. This will also increase your reputation of being a reliable figure. Meanwhile, building trust among them will enhance work-productivity, information-sharing, and team unity.

To be able to put this trait into practice one must observe the other principles mentioned in this e-book, especially the following: Honesty, integrity, empathy, and communication. Below are simple tips on how to gain trust and how to build it among your people:

1. Don't be the root of gossip: As a leader, you should maintain the peace and the quality of information circulating within your organization. Discourage the circulation of false information among your people by preventing the formation of gossip. Show your dedication to the truth by focusing on hard facts and by studying the information that you receive. People are more likely to trust you if they see that you are focused on approaching matters objectively. If you hear your co-workers and subordinates talking behind each other'

backs, remind them that they should minimize idle conversations which will not contribute to anybody's progress.

2. Respect matters of confidentiality: Learn when and to whom you should disclose confidential matters. Although openness is one way of gaining your people's trust, you should learn when to filter company secrets and how to stay silent about personal issues. If people around you observe that you are careless about disclosing confidential matters, they might hesitate to share their concerns about serious issues with you. If your organization shares a confidential matter with you, ask them first if you have the authority to share it with your team members. If they limit the number of people you can share the information with, make sure that you don't go beyond the limitations which they've set. Likewise, if your subordinates and your co-workers share a personal issue with you-- such as family problems or personal secrets, avoid talking about it with other people regardless of whether or not they give you the permission to do so. As a leader, you should keep your professionalism intact at all times.

3. Say what you mean and mean what you say: Practice having a word of honor. Never say things out of the blue just for the sake of having an opinion on a certain matter. If you make a commitment, make sure to see it through until you have completed it. It doesn't matter if it's a small task such as attending a subordinate's birthday, or something as serious as promising to volunteer for

overtime at work. Show people that you can be trusted by proving to them that you are capable of doing what you say you will do.

> "NOT ALL GREAT LEADERS ARE CREATED EQUAL, BUT ALL GREAT LEADERS SHARE COMMON CHARACTERISTICS"

PRINCIPLE 23

ROLE MODEL CREDIBILITY: AIM TO BE A LEADER AND NOT A TYRANT

There is a fine line between being feared and being respected. As someone who holds the power of leadership, you must know the difference between being a leader and being a tyrant. A true leader should serve as a role model for self-motivation among his people. By stepping into the role, you have to bring influence to the people around you in a manner that will make them want to do better for themselves and for the people around them. However, don't pressure yourself into becoming a flawless superhero figure in order to gain their admiration. Instead, consider yourself as a life coach who teaches others to improve themselves by using yourself as a positive example. By being a role model, you show the people around you that bringing a positive impact to one's self and to the world is possible for anybody. Below are tips on how to become an effective role model:

1. Be confident and content with who you are: Don't hide your flaws and the mistakes you have done in the past. Instead, use these as tools to show people how you were able to overcome the obstacles which were brought into your life by internal and external forces. Let them know them how it had helped you become a better person today. Treat your past insecurities and mistakes as hurdles which you had to overcome. The proof that you are here today reading this e-book is proof that you are continuously learning to improve yourself.

2. Don't be angry: Never use this emotion to intimidate people. Don't raise your temper or your voice if you want people to listen to you. As mentioned in the principles concerning communication and eloquence, you should raise your point and the clarity of your message instead.

3. Be strong enough to stand on your own so you can support others: As a figure who serves as your people's guide, you must have the capacity to help others during moments of difficulty. For this, you should combine the principles of personal awareness, integrity, and self-discipline to develop emotional, spiritual and mental strength. No matter how competent your team is, you have to remain as the main source of support and motivation for everyone in order to maintain their drive for an efficient work-performance. Consider the confidence they have in your leadership as a binding instrument of the whole team. As a leader, your very existence is one of the main foundations of your team's unity.

PRINCIPLE 24

INITIATIVE: BE COURAGEOUS ABOUT TAKING THE FIRST STEP TO GET THINGS DONE

Initiative is the ability to initiate action. As a leader, you must provide your team the initial push that will propel them to get things done. This enhances your team's synergy and output quality. When you take the first step in getting a certain task done, you guide your team into the right direction of accomplishing it. This will aid you in keeping your team members working toward one goal in the same pace and through the same approach. When a leader is able to take the initiative accordingly, confusion and misdirection among your team members are less likely to occur. Below are tips to enhance your leadership initiative:

1. Don't be passive: Instead of waiting for the right moment to react, create the right moment to act. Take the first step to solve the problems at hand and don't simply rely on other people to get things done. There will be times when you will have to step out of your comfort zone to set things into motion. For example: You are pressed for time to complete a project with your group. On the day before the deadline, one of your team members has failed to show up at work due to a personal emergency. All your team members are occupied doing their assigned tasks and you are now short of one person. Instead of standing on the side or wasting your time to look for a replacement, take the initiative to fill in his shoes. Set

aside excuses such as pride or anxiety. Get ready to be involved in circumstances which you may not have foreseen getting into in order to meet your objectives.

2. Be courageous, not foolish: Being courageous means overcoming your fear in order to get things done. Never confuse it with lack of fear and lack of proper judgment. Having the courage to take the first step doesn't mean that you should start diving head-first without thinking about the consequences of your action. Consider the things that might be put at risk before you choose a certain course of action. Imagine how it will affect the people involved and how it could possibly improve or further worsen the situation.

3. Keep an eye out for improvements: Find ways to make things better. Don't let complacency take over you just because circumstances are stable or are in a positive state at the moment. Make it a habit to see the potential for growth in every person and circumstance. To do this, you must apply the principle mentioned in this e-book about respect: You must learn to recognize the significance of everything around you in order to push it to its full potential. When you continue to seek improvement in everything, you are more likely to create concrete ideas which will lead to progress. This will give you guidance in taking your initiative to the right direction.

PRINCIPLE 25

GENEROSITY IN WISDOM: SHARE YOUR KNOWLEDGE AND EXPERIENCES

As a leader, it is important to know that generosity is about giving your best abilities into your work and not on actual donation of material things. You must do everything you can for the sake of your people and for the completion of the tasks at hand. You must give your best in order to achieve the best. This means that you should be able to share your secrets about your best skills and abilities among your people in order to improve the whole team. Use your wisdom as a tool to guide your team through the challenges ahead of them.

To be able to put this trait on generosity into practice one must observe the other principles mentioned in this e-book, especially the following: Creativity, a winner's mindset, communication, and eloquence. Below are tips on how to effectively impart your knowledge among your team members:

1. Be a teacher: Consider the people in your team as both your group mates and your apprentices. Share your knowledge and experiences in a way that can enhance their own skills and abilities. Be creative in your teaching techniques to keep your group members interested. Your technique can be something as simple as sharing your experiences with them during light-hearted

conversations. It can also be done through a more direct approach of holding group workshops. However, always remember that the objective of your extended leadership role as a teacher is limited to guiding. Avoid spoon-feeding your people because it may impair their ability to function alone in the long-run.

2. Give hands-on drills: Knowledge is nothing without understanding and proper application. Encourage your people to incorporate the lessons which you've taught them into their own skills and abilities. Give them drills on how to apply your teachings during the execution of actual tasks. This will sharpen both their logical and technical abilities at an individual level. This will also reduce the risk of actual work blunder as the drills will serve as a trial-and-error stage. Brief training sessions that mimic the hands-on work environment will give them time to adjust their individual approach to the new knowledge which they've acquired.

3. Don't be greedy: Keep an open and generous state of mind. Share new things you have learned to your team mates. Don't feel or think that you are being robbed off of your years of studies and experiences every time you share a part of your knowledge to your people. When you are a leader, your knowledge isn't yours alone. Be confident that no one can steal your achievements. Your abilities and skills will not be decreased if you share it to the people around you. Rather, it can even enhance your leadership strengths through frequent

application. Teaching is a good way to enhance your memory retention and your ability to innovate your approaches in applying your skills and knowledge.

> "THE ATTITUDE OF YOUR TEAM WILL RARELY BE BETTER THAN THE ATTITUDE YOU'RE DEMONSTRATING"

PRINCIPLE 26

OPTIMISM: BE THE BEARER OF POSITIVITY

Being an optimistic leader helps you to look at circumstances and people in a more positive manner. Scientific studies show that people who have an optimistic outlook in life have lower stress levels, less chances of developing psychological illnesses, and are generally healthier mentally, emotionally, and physically. By being an optimistic leader, you are able to cope with difficult situations for longer periods of time. It will also enhance your ability to come up with more effective problem-solving approach.

According to psychologists and public speakers, an optimistic image and a positive vibe are likely to attract more people. As a leader, not only will this positive energy make you more likable, it will also help you stand out among your people. This contributes to the level of trust and respect your subordinates and co-workers have for you. Below are tips on how to become a more optimistic leader:

1. Learn how to look at the brighter side of things: Learning how to look at the positive side of circumstances will help you identify hidden opportunities in the midst of difficult situations. Encourage your people to share the same positive outlook. Encourage them to pay attention to the good news about your organization and your society. Then, use these good news as study materials on how it can help improve your organization

and your team's overall work performance. Observe how things went right and what are the factors that helped the circumstances lead to a positive direction. By looking at positive news more inquisitively, you and your team are able to have an optimistic outlook during your learning process. It will also enhance your problem-solving abilities and help everyone have a more optimistic mindset.

2. Show enthusiasm: Little things like having a cheerful expression and an energetic demeanor are more likely to encourage people to get involved with the tasks at hand. Instead of putting up a serious and stressed out expression on your face every time a task is waiting to be accomplished, show eagerness and appreciation. Even though your people may not start out having the same feeling of enthusiasm for the job, they will eventually develop a sense of appreciation for it. A leader's positive vibe can uplift the mood of an entire team as it gives them the feeling of having an accommodating and approachable authority to whom they can turn during times of difficulty.

3. Stay alert: Alertness shows that you have the energy to get the job done. Take care of your health and make sure that you get enough rest before dealing with the tasks at hand. Enhanced physical senses contribute to a sharper and more reactive mind. Your alertness also determines the pace of your work performance, which in turn, are often imitated by your team mates. Team members tend to take their leader's work-pace and

approach as hints on how they should do their part in accomplishing the job. By showing that you have an alert and energetic demeanor towards your job, you are setting the standards of a fast-paced work-performance for the entire team.

"A SENSE OF HUMOR IS PART OF THE ART OF LEADERSHIP, OF GETTING ALONG WITH PEOPLE, OF GETTING THINGS DONE."

PRINCIPLE 27

HUMOR: TAKE OPTIMISTIC LEADERSHIP ONE STEP FURTHER

You cannot apply this principle without putting the previous principle of optimism into practice first. You must learn to see the positive side of circumstances in order to have a tactful sense of humor. You don't have to be a natural comedian to make laughable jokes. However, knowing how to look at the humor in stressful situations will help both you and your team to enjoy working on tasks together. A leader who has a good sense of humor which his people can relate to can build a sense of familiarity and comfort in his work place.

At an individual level, humor enhances wit. By finding the humor in things, you incline your mind to naturally perceive situations in a more creative and playful manner. It can sharpen your mind and lower your stress levels at the same time. Below are tips to enhance your sense of humor as a leader:

1. Forgive yourself: Accept your mistakes and learn from them. Instead of being psychologically and emotionally weighed down by a setback, use it as a learning material. Likewise, don't dwell too much on sad and awkward situations.

2. Don't be sarcastic: Although having a sense of humor shows how quick-witted a person can be, you should avoid using sarcasm to bring people down or to prove your point. Sarcastic humor can be more hurtful than laughable. Be aware that not everyone has the same

level of wit and tolerance to listen and reply to sarcastic jokes. If you have issues about certain matters that you want to express, it is best if you address those in a more professional and direct manner.

3. Avoid performing pranks: Avoid performing jokes on others that may result to violence or extreme mood swings. Don't use other people's emotions as a source of amusement. This is a highly unprofessional way of being humorous. The victim of the prank may or may not show proof of feeling offended, but it will give them an impression that you have little respect for their feelings. Stick to witty verbal humor instead of resorting to dark and insensitive practical jokes.

4. Laugh: You don't always have to put up a stern attitude and a serious aura to be an effective leader. By showing people the lighter side of your emotions, you are more likely to gain their empathy. Don't be afraid to look silly or be the first person to crack a joke in a tense situation.

5. Pick the right timing: Having a sense of humor is a good way to lighten up stressful or depressing situations. However, it also requires tact. Read the atmosphere before you crack a joke. Choose the right time, place, and people before you say your jokes. Even though a situation may feel really tense, there are moments when we would have to let the moment pass instead of attempting to break it through humor. You should especially avoid cracking jokes in the middle of serious work presentations, team-brainstorming sessions, and reflections.

> "CHARISMA AND CHARM WILL INSTANTLY HELP TO CONVEY THE PASSION YOU HAVE AND TO GET PEOPLE ON BOARD"

> "Each person has their own code of conduct. Let everyone see what you stand for"

PRINCIPLE 28

TRANSPARENCY: LET PEOPLE SEE THROUGH YOUR HONESTY

Although honesty and transparency may sound synonymous, they are two different traits which must be possessed by a genuine leader. Honesty is a trait that you build internally. Meanwhile, transparency is something that only the people around you can judge. Transparency is the level of openness which people perceive that you are giving them. You can be an honest person, but without the right display of transparency, people may still have difficulties trying to get to know you. This can lead to wrong judgments and doubts about your credibility as a leader.

Transparency is important in gaining people's trust. This leadership principle must be observed hand in hand with integrity. You cannot be open about your deeds and your identity if people perceive that you are not consistent in possessing both traits. Lack of good background and present work performance may only harm your reputation if those are all that you can show about yourself to people. Below are tips on how you can become a more transparent leader to your team:

1. Be accessible: Your availability to answer professionally to your people's needs display your openness and dedication as a leader. Having an accommodating personality shows that you value and respect the people around you. It also shows that you are not doing

anything worth hiding from their eyes when you are outside of your workplace.

2. Be more sociable: You don't have to deprive yourself of personal privacy by being a people-person at all times. However, if you are the quiet and socially withdrawn type of person, you have to step out of your comfort zone when the occasion requires it. Take time to get to know your acquaintances, especially the members of your organization. As they share things about themselves, try to do the same things during conversations. Share a few relevant details about your career background, your interests, and your experiences.

3. Share the big picture: When an issue which concerns your team arises, inform them immediately. Respect the right of the individuals who are involved in a situation to stay informed. Even if there is some information that you may be prohibited from circulating due to corporation confidentiality, it is your team members' right to at least have an idea on the bigger picture of the circumstances at hand. This will help you find solutions to arising conflicts easier because more people will have an idea what kind of obstacles are waiting ahead.

4. Explain the details: If you have the authority to share information about certain issues that may be crucial to your team, keep it as precise and concise as possible. Never feel lazy about discussing the little details that affect the overall issue. As a leader, it is your duty to

assure the quality of information being received and processed by your team. By doing so, you are promoting the circulation of accurate information among your people.

> "A LEADER CAN CREATE A VISION AND PROVIDE DIRECTION. A TEAM IS LOST WITHOUT A LEADER"

PRINCIPLE 29

FOCUS: DIRECT YOUR ATTENTION WHERE IT IS NECESSARY

Focus, as a verb, is defined by Oxford Learner's Dictionaries (2016) as "to give attention, effort, etc. to one particular subject, situation or person rather than another". Or, as stated in its secondary definition, "to adapt or be adjusted so that things can be seen clearly; to adjust something so that you can see things clearly". Although both definitions are correct, the latter is better deserving of attention than the former.

Due to the dynamism required in effective leadership, a leader should be able to give his attention on more than two things at once. Although prioritizing affects the pace of how fast an individual shifts his attention from one matter over another, this should not result into canceling out your perception of importance on the other things at hand. Thus, in synchronization with the multitasking nature of leadership, focus should be understood as the ability to direct attention with clarity where it is needed. It is not about blocking temptations to accomplish a singular task at once. Focus is the ability to work despite recognizing that there are distractions around you. Below are tips to enhance your focus as a dynamic leader:

1. Don't limit your focus on the prize: Looking forward to reaping your rewards is a good way to motivate yourself and your team into finishing a task. However, looking too far ahead diverts your attention from the things that you should focus more on at present. Make sure that

you are giving as much attention on the quality of your performance as much as you look forward to receiving your long awaited rewards.

2. Don't confuse pondering with focusing: Focus requires clarity and direction. Meanwhile, to ponder means to let your thoughts wander to different possibilities and subject matters with little concern on your objectives. An example of pondering is the act of brainstorming about ideas you can discuss for your board meeting. On the other hand, an example for focusing is the act of suggesting concrete solutions that may solve the conflict which is being discussed during the board meeting.

3. Practice fast-thinking: Being a fast-thinker enables you to be a better decision maker. Adjust the pace of your decision-making skills to improve your ability to divert your attention from one issue to another. This will help you handle logical and technical multitasking with more accuracy and efficiency. In order to enhance your thinking pace, engage in concentration-enhancing drills and puzzle games during your free time.

4. Learn how to catch your own attention: Study the quality of things or circumstances that capture your attention and use it to enhance your focus on the tasks at hand. For example, if you are a highly visual-oriented person who gets attracted towards bright colors easily, consider incorporating visual aids in your work or study tools. If you're the type of person who learns faster through your auditory skills, use read-aloud settings to learn or

review your textual materials. This way, you'll be able to engage your attention into important things for longer periods of time.

"LAY OUT THE PATH YOU INTEND TO FOLLOW TO COMPLETE THE OBJECTIVE"

PRINCIPLE 30

PUNCTUALITY: LEARN TO VALUE TIME AND MEET YOUR DEADLINES

Punctuality is the ability to deliver results and act on the right time. Being punctual displays your commitment to your responsibilities. It also shows how seriously you honor your words and how much you respect the people who wait for you or for your outputs on the designated time. When you show an exemplary quality of being punctual, your team mates are more likely to do the same. They will not take project extensions for granted and they will be keener in turning over expected results on or before their deadlines. Below are simple tips you should apply every day to make punctuality a habit:

1. Stay organized: The key to getting things done on time is organization. Find a tool for schedule organization which works best for you. Learn to schedule your activities and commitments habitually. If you are the type of person who is attached to hand-held gadgets, consider using organizer-apps and alarms to remind yourself of important tasks and appointments. If you are the type of person who prefers to write down things in a more traditional manner, try using pocket notepads instead of using bulky notebook organizers. Notebook organizers may seem fancy, but they are less convenient to carry around due to their size and weight. Meanwhile, pocket notepads are easier to carry around as you can easily draw it out from your own pocket shirt or pants

even when you're in the middle of talking or walking. Notepads also double as note slips which you can tack onto boards or post with refrigerator magnets in case you want to leave reminders for others.

2. Learn to apologize for being late: It doesn't matter whether it was an event a subordinate invited you to, or if it was an appointment you have with your boss. Always apologize if you arrive late for any occasion. It doesn't matter how long or short you have kept them waiting. If you arrive past the designated time, acknowledge your own lateness and let them know that you didn't mean to keep them waiting. It would be better if you keep your apology short so you can move on to more productive topics of discussion. Only explain the reason for your late arrival should they ask for it or if you feel that it is necessary. However, don't be over-dramatic with your excuses and keep your reason simple.

3. Take your commitments seriously: Never agree to submit a project if you are not absolutely certain that you can deliver it on time. Likewise, never make promises about attending an event if you aren't certain that you can show up. Sometimes, no matter how much we schedule certain tasks, emergencies may arise. These emergencies may demand more of your time in order to be accomplished. It could clash with another task scheduled closely to it. In order to avoid this, keep yourself away from making impromptu commitments when you have another one still pending on your list. Finish your responsibilities one

at a time so you can avoid commitment conflicts in your schedule. Allocate breaks in between your schedule to give leeway for emergency cases.

"NO ONE WILL CARE MORE THAN YOU DO. NO ONE WILL WORK HARDER THAN YOU DO. DEMONSTRATE HOW IMPORTANT THE PROJECT IS TO YOU"

PRINCIPLE 31

DISCERNMENT: BE KEEN ON OBSERVING THE DETAILS

Discernment is the ability to read beyond the superficial. This is particularly important for leaders because they are individuals who are in charge of overseeing the performance and outputs of their people. When you are able to see through people's motives and through the surface of situations, you are able to anticipate and prevent disasters and conflicts from arising.

In order to develop this ability, you must keep a keen eye on people, things, and circumstances that are part of your daily life. Below are tips on how to become a discerning leader:

1. Know the difference between connotation and denotation: Denotation refers to the literal meaning of a word found in the dictionary. Meanwhile, connotation refers to the things associated with it. These are often figures of speech used in both literary works, or puns and innuendos used in humorous everyday-conversations. When you write or review documents, people tend to be more specific and use words according to their literal meaning. However, as a leader you should be keener in reading connotations, especially when dealing with the people in your own team. You should learn to read between the jokes and the choice of words a person uses in different types of conversations. By understanding a person's way of conversing, you will be able to pick up

hints on their personalities, knowledge and experiences. For example, if a person has a limited understanding of a subject, he may resort to using flowery words and metaphors in order to hide his lack of knowledge on the matter. If you were talking with such a person, you would be able to see right away that he is prone to deceiving people. You'd be able to conclude that he is somebody you should avoid from trusting with confidential matters.

2. Observe the atmosphere: It is especially important to read the atmosphere when you are in between a serious situation that involves a lot of people. Learn to observe how the people around you interact with each other. Notice the tone of their voice, choice of words, and body language. For example, you are presenting a business proposal to a room full of investors. As you speak, you may see somebody yawn, another person lean back on his chair, and another frown as you click to the next slide. By noticing their body language, you already know that you should change the pace of your presentation or come up with an alternative proposal that will be more appealing to them. If you hadn't noticed their reactions and just kept talking without making any changes during your proposal, you would have simply wasted your own efforts and your investor's time without a chance of success.

3. Observe the different angles of every situation: Study the positive and the negative side of every action and circumstance. Look at how the smaller details affect the

bigger picture of every situation. For example, you are assigned to accomplish a certain task with your team. As everybody does their share of work, you notice how one person seems to take too long accomplishing their assigned task. By noticing this, you are able to track right away who is having difficulties coping up with the rest of the team. Through discernment, you'll be able to find solutions or change strategies according to the needs of the person or the situation at hand.

"ALWAYS BE THINKING ABOUT THE FUTURE. KNOW YOUR VISION AND BE AWARE OF CHANGES IN THE MARKET."

PRINCIPLE 32

GOAL-SETTING: IDENTIFY SHORT TERM AND LONG TERM GOALS

Setting goals give you and your team a more defined direction towards your objectives. It enhances your strategic-thinking and ability to focus. A leader who knows how to set goals objectively for himself and for his people are capable of enhancing team unity and task-specific work performance. By setting long term and short term goals, you and your team are able to focus your time and effort toward achieving significant results with more clarity and efficiency.

Goal-setting also helps you evaluate the level of your success and the effectiveness of your strategies. By setting time-bound objectives, you can determine if the pace of your performance is in sync with your plans. If you lag behind from your planned time frame, or if your current position is far from the development you have expected, then you'd easily know that a change in your strategies is needed. Below are simple tips to enhance you goal-setting skills:

1. When creating goals break them down from long term to short term and even daily. Example; when running projects that are a year long i break them down in 90-day blitz and then month to month and week from week. By doing this you are able to stay on course and adjust when necessary to make sure your staying on track.

2. Be specific: Look at your goals in an objective manner by understanding the details. Understand why you want

to achieve it and how you intend to achieve it. A few basic questions that you should ask yourself (and your team-- should you be working in groups) when setting a serious goal are: What do I/we exactly want to happen? Where do I/we need to be? How long before I/we can get there? What are my/our motives for setting this goal? How will it benefit me/us? Who else will I/we be taking along with me/us on the journey to achieve it?

3. Identify the needs of each goal: Find out who are the right people who can help you achieve it. Assess if the skills, abilities, and resources you currently have with you are enough to get you started on achieving your goal. If you don't possess all the material and non-material resources necessary to attain your goal at present, consider the alternative routes to achieve it. You can also break down your long term goals into smaller portions: Make achieving the necessary tools and resources for your long term goals a part of your short term ones. By breaking down your goals into several steps, even the most complicated long term goals will become more attainable.

4. Stop making excuses: Remove whatever internal borders you may be putting on yourself or on your team whenever you are deciding on your goals. These internal borders include fears, doubts, and personal bias. Stop telling yourself why you can't achieve a goal. Instead, focus on how you can achieve it. Go over the first and second tip mentioned above until you overcome your personal excuses.

5. Create back-up plans: Synchronize your strategies with your time frame and your abilities. However, never discount the possibilities of fall backs from occurring as you work your way towards your goals. Remember that there are both internal and external factors that can disrupt the pattern of your plans. List down alternate solutions that will get you back on track in every step should an obstacle lead you away from your intended direction.

"TO BE AN EFFECTIVE LEADER, YOU MUST FIRST BE A LEADER OF YOU"

PRINCIPLE 33

LEVELHEADEDNESS: USE LOGIC AND RATIONALE ON EVERYDAY DECISIONS

Levelheadedness helps a leader make sensible decisions through the use of logic and rationale. Logic is the science of reasoning which validates inferences and the interrelation of information. These information may be in the form of facts, figures, and phenomena. Meanwhile, rationale is the explanation behind how these information are controlled or perceived though certain cultures and principles. Levelheadedness is impossible without the combined use of the two. This is because logic is required for the establishment of a reasonable judgment. Rationale, in turn, proves how logic exists in the said judgment through formation of statements and arguments. Through rationale, people around the decision-maker are able to determine the significance of his decisions.

Being a levelheaded leader requires the application of the previous principles mentioned in this e-book, particularly the following: professionalism, focus, and discernment. Below are tips on how to develop levelheadedness:

1. Act upon your logic: Recall the tips mentioned in the 24th principle of this e-book which focuses on initiative, and then incorporate it with this tip. Upon having a logical discourse with yourself or with your team, make sure to put your logic into good use through actual application. The only way to prove the effectiveness and accuracy of a rationale is through concrete trials and

keen observation for errors. Put your plans into action and don't get stuck in the brain-storming phase.

2. Don't limit your judgment to a single type of evidence: Using figures as basis of performance level is a rational and specific way to evaluate results. However, a lot of people tend to narrow their judgment on present issues when they focus on numbers alone. This is a particularly common issue among corporate organizations. For example, your finance department gives your marketing department the challenge of increasing sales by twenty-five percent. Instead of focusing on the quality of their marketing strategies, the marketing department focuses on gathering potential market pool to meet the quota as soon as they possibly can. They are able to reach the required twenty-five percent sales increase, quickly. However, they were not able to maintain the sales index after two months as they did not carefully target specific consumers who are in need of the product which their business offers. They simply hoarded to meet the figures. Being a levelheaded leader, you can avoid similar mistakes by studying the different factors and consequences that affect your decisions and actions.

3. Maximize the use of your common sense: Being a levelheaded person doesn't have to be complicated. In fact, one of a levelheaded leader's tasks is to simplify what may seem challenging for his people to understand. Aside from using your expertise to understand and explain the logic behind your decisions, don't forget to apply basic common sense to simplify your rationale.

This way, you program your mind to see logic and rationality as a simple task which can be applied to everyday tasks. Eventually, levelheadedness will become a habit that would stick to your character and your state of mind.

"A GREAT LEADER CAN RELY ON EXPERIENCE AND INTUITION TO FIND THE BEST SOLUTION"

PRINCIPLE 34

FAIRNESS: TREAT THE MEMBERS OF YOUR WORKFORCE JUSTLY

Fair leadership is not about treating everyone equally or with the same level of conformity. It's about treating every individual justly. A just leader bases the kind of recognition he gives to his people according to the value of their performance and contribution to the organization. This requires a leader to treat each member of his team uniquely and appropriately. He must respect and recognize the differences in strengths, skills, and weaknesses of every individual in his team. By cultivating fairness within your organization, you are promoting a harmonious and healthy competition among your coworkers and subordinates. Below are tips on how to practice fair leadership:

1. Cultivate a sense of assurance among your people: To carry out this tip successfully, you must apply the principles of respect, integrity, trust-building, and open-communication. It is not enough for you to treat people accordingly. You have to show and assure them that you are, indeed, treating each one of them with fairness through concrete ways of leadership. If people feel that they are neither appreciated nor recognized enough as part of the team, they will think that they are not being treated fairly even if that isn't the case. They are more likely to lose confidence in your leadership and in their own abilities if they don't feel assured that

they are being given what they are due. Assure them that every member in your team is being treated fairly by establishing specific rules and processes for giving rewards and penalties. Have an open discussion about the factors that may result to exceptions of the said rules to avoid envy and misunderstandings from occurring.

2. Remember that not every person deserves the same amount of recognition: Fairness is all about balance. Give attention to every member of your team as needed. Don't coach somebody who already knows what he's doing. After acknowledging him for a job well done, shift your attention to those who need more of your guidance. Check the different needs and weaknesses of every person in your team. Do what you can to help them overcome it in a way that will contribute to the positive performance of the whole group. When somebody in your team makes a mistake, don't discriminate him or punish him beyond the penalties that he deserves.

3. Treat feedback from your people with equal significance: When you treat the feedback and concerns expressed by your people with equal significance, you not only display fairness, but respect and professionalism as well. Show them that you recognize the uniqueness that they bring to the group by listening to the feedback that they each contribute during discussions and peer evaluations. During open discussions and board meetings, always give each person a chance to express their concerns and suggestions. If there are too many people in your

team and you have limited time to accommodate their concerns, break the team into subgroups where they can discuss and synthesize whatever feedback they may have.

"A LEADER IS ONLY AS EFFECTIVE AS HIS OR HER FOLLOWERS WHO CARRY OUT THE DECISIONS MADE AND THE TASKS ACCOMPLISHED"

PRINCIPLE 35

INQUISITIVENESS: HAVE A CRITICAL EYE FOR INFORMATION

Inquisitiveness is the curiosity to learn more. As an inquisitive leader, you should have the curiosity to understand matters at a deeper level in order to find the root of a conflict and the different approaches to solve it. You must also put into practice the principles on open-mindedness, winner's mindset, initiative, and discernment in order to apply inquisitiveness productively into your leadership. Below are tips to enhance your inquisitiveness:

1. Ask relevant questions: Although inquisitiveness is a trait you should put into practice in order to establish a natural desire for learning, you should remain tactful and objective as a leader at all times. Being randomly curious and asking questions about things that may be insignificant to the matters at hand will make you appear nosy and annoying to your team mates. Keep your questions relevant by relating your queries with the objectives of the discussion or the situation. Before voicing out a question, ask yourself first how having it answered could contribute to the discussion.

2. Use deductive and inductive reasoning: Practice applying different types of scientific and logical reasoning to make sense out of your queries, especially when you're the one pondering over the possible answers for your questions. Deductive reasoning applies general theories to specific

matters in order to arrive at a conclusion.

3. For example: A good leader is a good follower. Susan is a good follower. Therefore, Susan is, or can be, a good leader. However, it is important to note that following the deductive pattern of reasoning can also lead to wrong generalizations. For example: Lack of experience leads to problematic work-performance. John has no experience at his job as a manager. Therefore, John will have a problematic work-performance. Applying only one kind of logic when reasoning out could result to bias and lack of sensibilities. This is why a leader should also be open about questioning and using different types of logic to figure out problems and situations. Inaccuracies can also occur in inductive reasoning. This counterpart of deductive reasoning begins with the observation of a specific case which is then used to formulate patterns. These patterns are then applied to generalizations. For example: Cleo is an employee from Jim's company. Cleo is an efficient employee. Therefore, all employees from Jim's company are efficient. These examples show that even scientific methods can lead to inaccurate results. When leaders apply logic to their curiosities, they are able to use their inquisitiveness to resolve matters with a more systematic and unbiased mindset.

4. Don't stop until you find the answers: The perseverance to find out the answer or the solution to a problem makes your curiosity lead to productivity. This combination of perseverance and the desire to learn helps in developing

your inquisitiveness even further. At the same time, it maximizes your capacity to assess situations which can be beneficial for your team and the whole organization.

> "YOUR VISION IS WHAT GIVES YOU YOUR GOAL. IT SHOULD BE WHAT GIVES YOU YOUR DRIVE TO SUCCEED AND MAKES THAT PASSION CONTA-GIOUS."

PRINCIPLE 36

CONSTRUCTIVENESS: CRITICIZE TO IMPROVE AND NOT TO DISCOURAGE

As a leader, it is important to extend constructiveness beyond putting projects and plans together. You must also apply constructiveness to your ideas and opinions, including how you express them. This is particularly important whenever you are voicing out criticisms toward your team members. Never use your words to harm or offend anybody, because this could lead to loss of skillful workforce and the decline of good-quality results. You must learn to use your opinions to improve your team's skills and overall performance.

In order to be successful at giving constructive criticism, you must apply the principles on respect, empathy, fairness, eloquence, and professionalism which have been mentioned in the previous chapters of this book. These principles particularly focus on tact and people-awareness. Remember that above all else, these two traits are the most important when communicating issues which may be perceived by others as sensitive subjects. Below are tips on how to give constructive criticism:

1. Be descriptive when voicing out your criticisms: Explain the details of why you ended with a certain review or conclusion about a team mate's behavior or work performance. For example, don't simply say "You're bad at this," or "your outputs are terrible". If you

simply end your criticism with a short and negative adjective, the receiver will feel offended and discouraged because they wouldn't know exactly what they did wrong. Say what exactly made a person's behavior or output disappointing to you. Give a brief but specific explanation on your expectations and which part of their action or work output failed to meet your standards. This way, they will be able to find out how to improve their behavior or their work performance so they don't commit the same mistake or offense again.

2. Focus on the objective: Focus on the behavior or the mistake of the person, and not at the person himself. Remember that constructive criticism is a form of behavioral assessment and performance evaluation. Don't say anything that will criticize a person's individuality or personality. Crossing the boundaries between professional and personal issues will cause more damage than improvement on the situation and the person. Stay professional by keeping your criticism focused on the mistake or offense which they have committed. Make it clear to them that you are not disappointed or angry at them, but at their actions or behavior.

3. Reinforce your suggestions, but don't impose: After giving your criticism, give suggestions on how the person can improve his behavior or his work performance. Always aim at improvement as you give your suggestions because this is what makes criticisms

constructive. However, avoid sounding too forceful or authoritative. Give a number of suggestions which they can choose from in a calm and enthusiastic manner.

"FOR A LEADER TO MAKE A DIFFERENCE, THEY MUST FIRST BECOME THE DIFFERENCE"

PRINCIPLE 37

ENCOURAGING NATURE: HAVE A NURTURING APPROACH IN LEADERSHIP

In order to make performance-enhancement and individual-improvement your objective, you must have a nurturing approach to leadership. A nurturing approach focuses on encouragement and personal growth. Through this approach, you are directing your guidance on how each individual in your group could improve their skills and abilities. This approach requires an encouraging nature so it can be applied effectively to your leadership style. In order to develop this nature, you should incorporate the principles mentioned in this e-book regarding optimism, generosity in wisdom, and constructiveness. Below are tips on how to have a nurturing approach in leadership:

1. Share words and thoughts of encouragement: Even if the words of encouragement may seem a little cliché for your liking, don't hesitate to share them to your team, especially during moments of difficulties. Tell them about your favorite inspirational books and movies. Post words of wisdom and motivation on your office tack board or memo board as often as you can every week so everyone can read them. You may also insert words of inspiration in between light-hearted discussions. It's a simple act, but it's still a form of sharing which shows your team that you care.

2. Use positive words and praises during introductions: Don't be bland when you introduce your team members to others. Put emphasis on their accomplishments or the positive side of their personality whenever you give a brief introduction of who they are. This will help them to feel appreciated and boost their confidence when facing new people. For example, instead of saying, "This is Johnny. He's my new secretary," say, "This is my efficient and optimistic secretary, Johnny. He was the one who booked my successful interview yesterday." Keep your introduction and compliment short and simple so you don't sound like you are bragging or exaggerating about your team member's abilities.

3. Be present: Show moral support to your team by being present during the most crucial moments or significant events. These crucial moments can be a group presentation during a board meeting, or an individual milestone such as a career promotion. This will help in boosting their confidence because they know that their leader is there to give them guidance and support.

4. Give lessons and not punishments: When you give penalties or punishments to a team member or a subordinate for their failure or mistake, they tend to become hostile or feel discouraged. Instead of focusing on making them feel how wrong they were, make them think about how they should make things right next time. For example, instead of issuing a memo for suspension, assign the offender to more work hours under the guidance of a dependable figure. Find alternative

ways on how they can improve their behavior or work performance. This way, you are able to utilize their skills and abilities for the benefit of the organization, as well as further bring out their potential.

> "LEADERS INSTILL CONFIDENCE. MAKING SOMEONE FEEL CONFIDENT IN THEIR ABILITIES IS A GIFT THAT AN EFFECTIVE LEADER PROVIDES"

PRINCIPLE 38

CONSIDERATION: GIVE A CHANCE TO THOSE WHO DESERVE IT

Consideration is the act of carefully thinking before finalizing a decision, usually to avoid offending or upsetting another person. Being a considerate leader is important to maintain the strength and the number of your workforce. A considerate way of thinking displays how well you can balance compassion with professionalism. If you don't possess the ability to balance these two traits, your people might feel under appreciated by you and the whole team. This could lead to their loss of enthusiasm to follow you and finish their assigned tasks. On the other hand, when you give them room for consideration, you boost their self-motivation and their trust in you.

To apply sensible consideration into your leadership style, you must practice it hand in hand with the following principles discussed in this e-book: empathy, open-mindedness, fairness, and encouraging nature. Below are tips on how to become a considerate leader:

1. Don't resort to penalties or punishments right away: Apply the principle of empathy and communication for this tip. Put yourself in the other person's shoes before you issue him a penalty for the mistake he had committed. Take into consideration the factors which had lead him into making the mistake. Give him a chance to explain before resorting to punishment. Lastly,

weigh if the penalty being given to him is justifiable or too harsh for the offense he had committed. If you think that the punishment is too severe, consider adjusting it accordingly.

2. Respect personal decisions: Sometimes, when teams commit certain conflicts and blunders, members reach a point when they make the final decision on whether or not they should stick to their commitments. Although it is your duty as a leader to keep the team united, you should never force a member to stay. This will only result to half-hearted work performance in the long-run. If a person makes a request for task reassignment or decides to tender a letter of resignation, you must respect their personal decisions. Consider the reasons for their action before declining their requests. Try to persuade them to the best of your professional abilities, but never impose on matters which only they should decide for themselves.

3. Offer your guidance or assistance: If somebody in your team lags behind in their work performance, extend your guidance. Give them a chance to do better at their job. If they reject your help, don't further impose as this could only make them feel that you're crossing their personal space. Still give them a chance to prove their abilities without your guidance. However, if there are no signs of improvement given the specific number of chances you have given them, then you should proceed with the appropriate course of action. Remember that being

a considerate leader has its limitations. The adjustments and the chances you give for your people should never put into compromise the whole organization's objectives.

> "THE REACTION YOU CHOOSE TO ADVERSITY WILL DETERMINE WHETHER OR NOT YOU GO ON TO SUCCESS OR MORE FAILURES AS A LEADER"

PRINCIPLE 39

PRACTICALITY: MAKE THE MOST OUT OF EVERY SITUATION AND AVAILABLE RESOURCES

Practicality is the ability to perceive the most reasonable decisions and make the most appropriate actions. Practical leadership allows you to weigh the risks and benefits of every action you take. It helps you find smart ways to get tasks done with less effort and stress. It minimizes the probable occurrence of errors and wastage of resources.

Below are tips on how to become a practical leader:

1. Don't ignore abnormalities: If you sense that something is not right about a situation or a process, investigate it right away. If you let these abnormalities pass your troubleshooting radar, it might grow into a bigger problem. Find the root of the abnormality in a situation and find ways to prevent it before it turns into a disaster. When you deal with issues while they are still small, you would have fewer difficulties to face in the future. You are also less likely to suffer from losses and damages because smaller problems tend to require less demanding solutions.

2. Avoid going beyond the allocated budget or resources: Practicality takes into account the value of both tangible and non-tangible resources. Utilize what you have to the best of your abilities in order to minimize expenses and task-related demands. For example, if you are given

a limited budget to finish a project, use your creativity in order to make the quality of the final output better than the cheap raw materials it was made of. If you are short of people to get a certain job done, try breaking it down into smaller assignments and re-aligning people to do each task. This way, the people in your team will be able to accommodate all the tasks that need to be accomplished without wasting time to search for an additional man power.

3. Make systematic follow-up a part of your leadership routine: Instead of waiting for confirmation from people if they have already done their assigned tasks, be the one to enforce update circulation and tasking follow-ups. This way, you minimize the risk of getting any tasks neglected. Your constant reminders and updates will help to keep your team members alert about the things which they need to accomplish. Make task follow-ups a regular part of your leadership routine to enhance task-focus and goal-assertiveness among your team members.

4. Practicality is about being reasonable: Being practical doesn't always mean choosing the more convenient path. Being a leader requires a certain amount of self-sacrifice through servitude. Always choose the more reasonable options for the sake of the team and the organization over your personal convenience. Remember that even if a task may have a simple demand, it may require more effort from your side in order to become effective. This is because being a leader, there are certain things that

you can do which your team members cannot. It may be due to authoritative or political reasons, or limitations on knowledge skills, or abilities.

"TO DEVELOP A VISION, A LEADER MUST LOOK WITHIN AND BRING OUT THAT VISION IN YOU FIRST"

PRINCIPLE 40

ENTREPRENEURSHIP: HAVE A BUSINESS-MINDED POINT OF VIEW ON DEVELOPMENT AND SUSTENANCE

According to the Concise Encyclopedia of Economics (2008), "Entrepreneurship is the process of discovering new ways of combining resources". Regardless of whether or not you are leading a business-oriented team, looking at things through an entrepreneurial point of view can help you become a more objective leader. Through an entrepreneurial perspective, you become more aware of the value of both tangible and non-tangible resources, and you learn to balance practicality with creativity. In turn, this balance will give you a more dynamic outlook at development and sustenance of excellent work performance and outputs.

For an effective implementation, this principle on entrepreneurial leadership must be observed hand in hand with the following principles: preparedness, creativity, open-mindedness, and practicality. Below are tips on how to develop an entrepreneurial mindset:

1. Familiarize yourself with the basics of marketing and economics: Marketing is the act of building people's awareness on your products and services. Meanwhile, economics is a social science focusing on the different systems and theories on how goods and services are allocated. When you understand the basics of marketing, you enhance your ability to empathize with the people

around you. It helps you perceive people's behavior and interests as tools to figure out their wants and needs. On the other hand, when you understand the basics of economics, you learn how to allocate both tangible and non-tangible resources in a manner that will be more beneficial to you, your team, and the whole organization. Through Economics, you understand how the manipulation, scarcity, and abundance of resources, can impact your organization in different aspects.

2. Invest certain resources for future gains: As mentioned in the introduction of this principle, these resources refer to both tangible and non-tangible assets. Non-tangible resources may refer to skills, knowledge, and time. Meanwhile, tangible resources may refer to money, tools, and other material things that can be utilized for your own wants and needs. Learn to allocate certain amounts of these resources for future use. This way, you are ensured that you'll be equipped with the right tools to be demanded by future challenges. Allocation of resources need not be complicated or financially related. For example, every time you allocate time and patience on guiding your team members, you are investing your efforts to develop your team's work performance. In turn, they are able to accomplish tasks more efficiently and produce results with better quality.

3. View competition as a challenge for growth and development: Entrepreneurs know that market competition is a threat to business opportunities. It calls for innovation and reconstruction of approach in order to

rise above the rest. Consider political and organizational competition in the same manner. Perceive competition as a challenge to improve internal growth and innovate your work performance. Continue to develop the strengths which you and your team currently possess in order to rise above the standards set by external forces.

"A LEADER WHO SEE'S LEADERSHIP DEVELOPMENT AS COMPETITION INSTEAD OF COOPERATION IS PART OF A TEAM THAT ISN'T GROWING AND SUCCEEDING"

PRINCIPLE 41

TEAM-ORIENTED MINDSET: MAKE TEAM GROWTH A PERMANENT OBJECTIVE

In order to be successful at being a leader, you must consider your people not just as subordinates, but as team mates as well. This is one of the distinct differences between a regular superior or a boss, and a leading superior or a team leader. Your strength and credibility as a leader largely depend on how well you can bind these diverse talents together in order to deliver high quality results. You must look at each member as individuals who add strength and support to the whole organization through their diverse skills and abilities.

In order to be successful at making team growth a permanent objective in your leadership, you should incorporate the principle of Respect and Selflessness into your approach. A team-oriented mindset always focuses on how a leader can contribute to the development of the whole team. His focus goes beyond producing excellent outputs and gaining personal recognition. Below are tips on how to become a team-oriented leader:

1. Learn together: Make sure that the whole team remains synchronized for the start until the end of every group assignment. Before accomplishing a certain group task, always get together to brainstorm ideas and clarify plans. This will assure you that every member of the team is briefed with the right amount of details before

getting involved with the task. After accomplishing the task, gather the members of your team once more and synthesize the lessons and realizations which everybody had acquired from every experience. This way, everybody gets to contribute a piece of their own knowledge to the whole group.

2. Create a power team within your team: Make a private list of the best or the strongest members of your team. However, as it had been emphasized in principle 34, you must treat each and every team member with fairness. As you make the list, avoid picking your personal favorites. The purpose of listing down your top strongest team members is to help you determine who among your team are most capable of handling difficult tasks. You can assign these top members to guide weaker members or the newcomers in the group. Making a list of who are the strongest and who are the weakest members of your group will also help in assessing who needs the most and the least of your guidance during task performance.

3. Keep things simple: Make policies and processes easy to understand. Establish work-performance systems that will make it easier for the new members of your team to cope up with the rest. This way, you'll spend less time focusing on newbie-orientation since the newcomers will get over the adjustment phase quicker. Establishing a specific system for different types of work-performance will also help in providing structured guides for both new members and weak members alike. The whole team

is more likely to move towards the same direction and in the same pace if they are aware of the patterns in which they should move along together.

"BEING LIKABLE ISN'T THE SAME AS BEING A PUSHOVER. HOLD PEOPLE ACCOUNTABLE, BUT BE FAIR"

PRINCIPLE 42

FRIENDLINESS: PUT A BORDERLINE BETWEEN BEING A LEADER AND BEING A BUDDY

Being approachable and accommodating are important traits of friendliness a leader must possess in order to gain their team's trust and loyalty. A leader must be able to apply the principles of humility, empathy, communication, and consideration to their leadership approach in order to create a friendly impression on your team. However, a definite line needs to be drawn between being an actual friend and being friendly. In order to do this, you must be aware of the definition of the two words: Friendliness is a behavior that gives people the impression that an individual is a pleasant and approachable person. Meanwhile, being a friend means engaging in a platonic relationship that requires a certain amount of actual personal familiarity.

As a leader, some things must be kept at bay in order to protect your reputation and the confidentiality which your position entails. To put it simply, you must avoid engaging in any relationship that goes beyond the professional scope of your leadership among your team. Below are tips on how to be a friendly leader without being perceived by your team mates as a personal buddy:

1. Always bring the topic back to the task objectives: You will notice a personal turn of conversation when your team members start to ask you questions about your

private life and when they start to share inappropriate jokes with you. When this happens, bring the topic back to professional matters so they are reminded that they are still talking to their leader. You may share personal wisdom and experiences during casual conversations as it may contribute to your team's confidence and personal growth. However, limit your sharing of personal information and sentimental opinions. If your team members get too comfortable being around you, they might start seeing you as their personal friend. If this happens, they will start expecting you to do personal favors for them and biases may arise at work.

2. Observe professional decorum when attending personal events: You can let your guard down and not talk about organizational matters when you are invited to important personal events by your team members. However, you must keep your behavior in check. The purpose of attending personal events is to show your open and accommodating nature to your team mates, not for you to lose yourself in all the fun. Don't get drunk, high, or get caught doing anything a leader is not supposed to be seen doing. Although you may not mean any offense, photos that may spread on social media may result to misunderstandings and bad impressions on your leadership.

3. Minimize impressions of scolding: Become a friendly leader by not creating a terrifying reputation for yourself among your team members. Instead of scolding a team mate, resort to a more calm approach of issuing

reminders and warnings. Even when you are issuing penalties, never resort to blaming or bashing. Always remember the tip on giving punishments in the principle on Fairness discussed in this e-book.

"A LEADER MAXIMIZES THEIR STRENGTHS AND ALLOWS THEIR TEAM TO HANDLE TASKS THAT THEIR WEAKER AT"

PRINCIPLE 43

DELEGATION: ASSIGN TASKS TO THE APPROPRIATE TALENTS

A leader holds the highest authority in a team but this doesn't mean that he should deal with all the hard tasks by himself. He has to break down tasks into smaller portions and sensibly distribute it between himself and the members of his team. This way, he can oversee the quality of the output and get the job done more efficiently. To be particular, when tasks are assigned to people with the right skills and abilities, there are lower risks of committing errors.

The duty of assigning tasks to appropriate people is called delegation. It's a strategy every leader should practice in order to prevent tasks and processes from being mismanaged. Through delegation, you are able to maximize your team's efficiency because tasks get accomplished faster while you hone your team's skills and abilities at the same time. Also, appropriate distribution of tasks breeds self confidence among people because they feel that they are being trusted to accomplish something as part of the team. Below are tips on how you can delegate tasks effectively:

1. Consider time lines: Before finding the right people to handle certain tasks, consider the target date for its completion. Some people may be skilled workers, but not all of them can get things done in a short period of time. If time is one of your main concerns, consider assigning the most tedious part of the group assignment to the

fastest workers in your team. Then, create a support group who can help them deal with the details to keep a good-quality result. Establish a regular inspection period for particularly time-constrained projects to inspect the progress of your team and the effectiveness of your delegation.

2. Think about the quality of your expected outputs: Consider the skills required to produce the expected result for every project. Identify the strengths and weaknesses of every member of your team. Study who among your members possess the skills to deliver the quality you expect in an output.

3. Balance the workload of your team: Don't keep assigning the same persons to do similar tasks repeatedly. If you don't balance the distribution of tasks among your team members, those who are getting more assignments than the others might end up with a lot of poor-quality or unfinished outputs. Meanwhile, those who are getting minimal assignments might slack off and take the hard workers for granted.

4. Work style: Although the leader is the one who establishes the control and the systems which his team should follow, he should always give consideration to every member's work style. Individuals may possess similar talents with other people in the team, but they may have different ways of getting things done. Study the compatibility of every member's work style before

forming subgroups for certain team assignments. This way, you can increase team synchronization and decrease risks of having ego conflicts during work performance.

"KNOW HOW TO BALANCE THE WHEEL OF LIFE. BECAUSE WHEN YOU GET A FLAT YOUR OUT OF BALANCE"

PRINCIPLE 44

BALANCE: INTEGRATE A HEALTHY WORK-LIFE BALANCE

Observing balance in the work place is crucial in promoting your team's harmonious relationship with their work and with one another. However, to keep this harmony consistent, a leader should extend this balance to his team's personal lives. Despite the boundaries between professionalism and friendliness, a leader should maintain a certain amount of concern over the fact that his members each have a life beyond their career. When your team members feel that they are in a nurturing and caring environment, you are able to raise their work satisfaction and their loyalty towards you and the rest of the team.

To be able to integrate a healthy work-life balance in your leadership, you must observe the following principles on schedule organization, empathy, creativity, and practicality into your leadership style. Below are tips to enhance work-life balance for you and your whole team:

1. Aim to promote your team's well-being: When you teach your team work-related lessons, make sure that it contains values which can enrich more than just their minds. When you boost their confidence and their motivation during your training and activities, you are able to contribute to their emotional, moral, and psychological well-being. It helps them feel appreciate the things they do under your leadership in many ways

because they see the significance it makes on both their career and personal development.

2. Decrease causes of work stress: Reduce long working hours and unclear task objectives to reduce the hassles of daily work tasks for everyone in your team. This can be done by taking a more systematic approach on task-organization and establishment of work execution processes. Meanwhile, integration of all the principles in this e-book will help you deal with your own leadership responsibilities more effectively with less hassle.

3. Increase work satisfaction: A consistent and proper delegation of tasks and establishment of a fair reward system will increase your team's work satisfaction. When people are happy with their career, they perceive a huge part of their personal accomplishment with enthusiasm. In turn, they are more likely to believe that they are capable of taking control over the different aspects of their life. This results to the creation of solid personal perception on the ability to attain work-life balance.

4. Integrate real-life practical sense into the team's work performance: Create practical systems based on real life which the members of your team can use to enhance their work-involvement and the quality of their results. Relate strategies to situations outside of work whenever you get the opportunity in team lectures and discussions. People are more likely to understand the strategies and the work processes which you establish if you use real life sense as teaching tools and examples. When people

perceive that both their personal and career experience can be integrated with each other, they become convinced that they are able to make the most out of the two main aspects of their life.

"LEADERS PROVIDE A VISION, MOTIVATION, AND DIRECTION WHILE ABSORBING MANY OF THE UNAPPEALING COMPONENTS OF A WORKPLACE TEAM"

PRINCIPLE 45

POLITICAL AWARENESS: LEARN THE RULES, CULTURE, AND THE RISKS OF HAVING AUTHORITATIVE POWERS

Along with the authoritative powers of leadership come the rules, challenges and risks of being in the position. If you are serious about being a leader and you intend to stay in the position for a long time, it is important for you to develop a strong sense of political awareness. By being politically aware, you are able to maximize the power that comes with your position. This awareness will also help you retain or develop your leadership status within the different groups that make up your social and career circle.

As you step into the position of being a leader, expect that there will be individuals and organizations who would criticize your decisions and actions despite your efforts of gaining their favors. The root for these criticisms may be personal-- such as envy and ego clashes, or professional-- such as career competition and organizational threats. To protect yourself from these types of destructive criticisms, you should integrate the following principles on organizational awareness, diplomacy, empathy, and having a winner's mindset into your understanding of political awareness. This will help you arm yourself with the skill and knowledge on political power-play. Below are tips on how to develop your political awareness:

1. Familiarize yourself with the organizational culture and hierarchy: Every organization has its own rules and set of etiquette. Study the norms and taboos inside the organization. Find out who are obliged to follow those standards and who are capable of changing and setting the standards. Use this organizational knowledge to understand how the people in your organization function and how it affects the performance of your team.

2. Recognize the threats to your leadership: Know the people and situations that can put your position at risk. If you notice that somebody is particularly hostile with you, or if you sense that something is not right with the way somebody is treating you, try to have a discussion with the person in question. It's better to have a face to face confrontation than to ignore these small ego clashes until it turns into a large conflict. Whether or not the person or organization decides to deny or face your confrontation, always adhere to the policies of professionalism and diplomacy. Never be the first one to display signs of offense because anything you say or do can be used against you during moments of political conflict.

3. Learn basic Psychology: Psychology is the study of the human mind and behavior. By having the basic knowledge on this scientific subject, you can enhance your leadership skills which deal with empathy such as communication, diplomacy and eloquence. It will be easier for you to analyze the intent behind a person's

manner of talking and body language patterns. As a result, you'll become less susceptible to deceptions and to other potentially malicious intents of those who perceive you as a threat.

"A LEADER THAT IS COMMITTED TO EXCELLENCE, HIS OR HER TALENTS ARE SHOWCASED IN THEIR LEADERSHIP ABILITIES"

PRINCIPLE 46

ASSERTIVENESS: HAVE A GO-GETTER ATTITUDE

Assertiveness is a trait of self-assurance often characterized by confident actions and manner of speaking. Psychologists consider this trait as a skill and mode of communication which anybody can develop with consistent practice. As a leader, it's a trait which must be observed as a principle to live by. If you make assertiveness a part of your natural character, you'd feel more confident in your decision-making skills and you'd have a better sense of enthusiasm to stand for your own beliefs. In order to effectively apply this principle into your leadership style, you must practice it hand in hand with the principles on initiative, optimism, goal-setting, and encouraging nature.

Assertiveness is also needed in establishing rules and systems in an organization. When a leader displays a strong sense of confidence in implementing rules and delegating assignments, he is able to propel his team members to take the appropriate action to accomplish tasks. It helps him promote team synergy for longer periods of time. Below are tips on how to be a more assertive leader:

1. Believe in the difference you can make: You can't be self-assured and you won't be able to do tasks confidently if you don't whole-heartedly believe in the things you say and do. In order to become a more assertive person, you have to raise the level of your self-respect. Never underestimate how your words and actions can affect

the people around you. Believe in the change that your actions and your objectives can make for your team and for the whole organization.

2. Don't be pushy: Being assertive should not be confused with being pushy. Assertiveness uses self-confidence to boost the persuasive appeal of an action or a message. In order to convince people to do or perceive things as you wish them to, you must remain tactful in emphasizing your point. Don't come off being unreasonably pushy, or else people might find you annoying. Balance your assertive attitude with professionalism. Only choose to escalate matters or resort to a more forceful mode of persuasion if you think that the situation is in dire need for it.

3. Give and receive feedback: Giving suggestions and expressing your ideas show that you are both mentally and physically present during team brainstorming. It's one of the ways you show to your team that you possess the energy and the enthusiasm to make things better. It also displays your willingness to get involved in group tasks. Meanwhile, listening to your team's feedback shows your eagerness to get other people involved in accomplishing the tasks with you. As a result, it boosts your team's sense of assertiveness as well. When everyone in your team is confident about their own skills and abilities, they are able to push beyond their known potential. This will help you raise your team's standards on work-performance excellence and output quality.

PRINCIPLE 47

RESPONSIBILITY: DON'T BE AFRAID TO BECOME ACCOUNTABLE

Being a leader requires a firm sense of responsibility. You have to possess the courage to stand up for yourself and for others. To be particular, you should have the mental, emotional, and psychological strength to withstand being held accountable for both positive and negative actions which your whole team makes. Although it may sometimes be a challenge to possess the amount of self-confidence required for responsible leadership, cultivating it in yourself will help you gain your team's trust and loyalty for longer periods of time.

Your team members are more likely to stay loyal to you during difficult situations because they know that they have a leader who isn't afraid to face the consequences in case things fail to turn out positively. They will also feel more at ease about following your decisions because they can see how confident you are in the things you say and do. As a result, they will be less likely to question you and disobey your orders. Below are tips on how to become a more responsible leader:

1. Use the word "I" when stating your own beliefs: Don't forget the principle on assertiveness which was discussed in this e-book. Make sure that your self-confidence emanates through your words and body language whenever you emphasize your points and explain your beliefs to others. Although using the pronoun "we" when representing your team is important because it shows your spirit as a team leader, it is better to use the

pronoun "I" when stating something personal. This not only shows your level of self-responsibility, but your sense of decisiveness as well. It shows people that you have the self-assurance required to share your own thoughts and ideas with others. It contributes to your eloquence and integrity.

2. Never pass the blame: When you pass the blame for your mistakes on other people, you show a lack of self-confidence and lack of honesty to your superiors and to your team mates. Admit to your mistakes and offer possible solutions. Accept the penalties that come with it while keeping your head held high and your self-respect intact. Consider your mistake as a lesson. Proudly show your team that taking responsibility for your own wrongdoings is an honorable act.

3. Consider every commitment you make as a promise: As it had been emphasized in the principles on honesty and integrity, you must honor every word you say. Never say anything that you cannot commit to doing. Get commitments done on the time and date you promised it to be accomplished. Remember that not honoring your own words is a form of dishonesty which can tarnish your integrity as a leader. Similarly, never leave a commitment incomplete because it will give others the impression that you're the type of person who will leave halfway through a journey at the moment it takes a difficult or demanding turn.

PRINCIPLE 48

PROBLEM-SOLVING: DON'T COPE WITH THE PROBLEM, SOLVE THEM

A curious and open mind will help a leader identify threats and challenges ahead of his team. It helps him keep a calm and rationale demeanor in the midst of trouble-shooting. This helps him formulate strategies to enhance his team's work performance during difficult situations. However, a leader's job doesn't end in team development and problem detection. He should keep his mind and his time open to create solutions for the problem.

Creating coping mechanisms for your team shouldn't become the main objective of your leadership. Don't simply pass through the problems that you encounter along the way. Eliminate the problems or turn them into opportunities by solving them together with your team. Apply the principles on creativity, levelheadedness, inquisitiveness, and practicality to your problem-solving methods so you don't get trapped in the trouble-shooting stage. Below are tips for effective problem-solving:

1. Face the problem: Identify the problem. Track its causes and study how it affects your team's work-performance and output. Never underestimate the severity of the damages it can cause. No matter how minor a problem may seem, it should be dealt with as soon as you possibly can. Don't pass the responsibility of solving it to anyone. As a leader, you should take the initiative to solve a

problem regardless of its severity. Involve your team to enhance their awareness and their problem-solving skills, but always oversee the process from the beginning until the end.

2. Relate the details to factual accounts: Make an information-based problem analysis. Conduct a data research. Compile your team's research and align your findings about the problem to the facts that you have gathered. Try comparing the problem to similar circumstances and try to identify a pattern. This way, you'll have solid facts to base your probable solutions on during your brainstorming stage.

3. Identify possible solutions: As you brainstorm for ideas, remind yourself of the principles on creativity and open-mindedness. Don't box yourself to tradition. Explore the conventional and non-conventional ways to solve the problem. If it is possible to use more than one solution and if it'll help you solve it more efficiently, do so. Make a list of the most applicable and the list applicable solutions. Consider the amount of time and the resources needed for each solution to be carried out.

4. Implement the solution: Apply the principle on task delegation when you break down the problem-solving operations into a team assignment. Assign team members who have dedication and perseverance to get the job done. Make sure that both the tangible and non-tangible tools required to carry out your problem-solving strategies are available. If something goes wrong

during the implementation process, adjust your strategy as necessary but be sure to proceed with the operation as soon as you possibly can. The longer that a problem is left unresolved, the bigger the damage it might cause.

"THERE IS MUCH TO BE LEARNED FROM THE GREAT LEADERS OF THE PAST SO MAKE SURE TO LEAVE A LEGACY"

PRINCIPLE 49

EXCELLENCE: SET STANDARDS AND EXCEED THEM

The most convenient way to make high-quality results and efficient work performance a standard, is by making excellence a permanent leadership objective. When a leader's mind is conditioned to aim for excellence, he sets a standard to achieve the best, through the best of his abilities. As a result, he finds creative ways to excel in almost everything he does. His definition of success is improvement and not perfection.

Although the two are closely associated with each other, "excellence" is different from "perfection". Excellence is a virtue characterized by undeniably high quality or standard of things, actions, or circumstances. On the other hand, perfection is the fixed set of standard which is observed to the smallest detail when things or actions are executed. Perfection may hinder a leader's open-mindedness, flexibility and creativity because he sets his mind to a particular standard. Meanwhile, excellence leaves room for constant improvement despite the already exceptional quality of a matter's present state. Below are tips on how to strive for excellence:

1. Set a standard and dare to exceed it: Establish work performance and output standards for yourself and for your team. Establish a status quo for different types of tasks and create a bonus system. The bonus system doesn't have to be a financially inclined reward. It

can be something as trivial as getting treated to free snacks and coffee, or something as big as a promotion endorsement. Then, make it a challenge for you and your people to exceed the status quo. The one who exceeds the standards the highest by the end of the week or the month gets the largest bonus which was agreed upon the establishment of the status quo.

2. Compete with yourself: Consider yourself as your worst rival. As a leader, seeking out other people to challenge may cause you unnecessary conflicts in your professional relationships. Instead of finding a personal competitor, use your previous accomplishments as a standard and compete with yourself. This way, you get to choose which fields you would like to raise your standards on, one skill at a time. You minimize the possibilities of ego clashes, envy, and misaligned comparisons with other people.

3. Encourage healthy competition among your team members: Although looking for personal competition between yourself and other leaders should be avoided due to unnecessary political complications, competition among your team members should be encouraged. Competition can help members strive to be the best asset of the team. However, as a leader, you must make sure that it doesn't turn into an unhealthy rivalry. Regulate the rules and the degree of the peer competition. Keep in mind the principle of fairness and treat every participating member justly. If you don't oversee the competition among your team, it can go out of control

and destroy the unity among the members. Always remind your people that the aim of the competition is to improve oneself for the betterment of the whole team.

"DEVELOPING A PASSION FOR YOUR CONVICTIONS INDICATE TO OTHERS THAT YOU HAVE CORE BELIEFS THAT CAN'T BE SHAKEN"

PRINCIPLE 50

CONSISTENCY: KEEP UP THE GOOD WORK

In order to see the long-term results of your leadership, you must be able to maintain your performance level consistent for a long period of time. You have to possess a never-ending trait of self-motivation and perseverance until you see that the quality you aim for turns into a standard among your team. This consistency in positive leadership performance should extend to your team members as well. As you constantly do your best to become a better leader, so should you continue to aim for your team's individual progress and overall group improvement.

Excellence and success should not be perceived as one-time goals, but as parts of your obligation as a leader. Consistent leadership entails a keen integration of the principles on self-discipline, personal awareness, assertiveness. You must put these principles into practice to help you develop the perseverance to pursue consistency. Remember that practice breeds familiarity, and familiarity breeds improvement. In turn, improvement results to excellence. Excellence can only be attained with continuous improvement. Therefore, a consistent leadership is a matter of repeating the cycle of practice, improvement, and attainment of excellence. Below are tips on how to be a consistent leader:

1. Never go below your standards: Integrate the principle on excellence for this tip. Conduct systematic quality check as part of your leadership routine. Evaluate every

output and compare its quality with the previous ones. Give your team and yourself the room to exceed your established status quo but never go below it. This way, you are able to maintain the quality of your outputs and there are less chances of abrupt decline in your team's work performance efficiency.

2. Implement the strategies and the plans you have agreed on: Putting plans into action is the best proof of team unity and the first step to productivity. Always make sure that your plans are put into action to maintain your team's level of productivity. Assign team members to oversee the implementation of those plans to assure that its every step is being implemented.

3. Never get tired of constant reminders: Repetition is the key to better memory retention. When you are able to remember important details better, you are less likely to overlook important tasks and information. Apply the principle of schedule-organization for this tip. Keep a record of your accomplishments and previous projects to keep track of your work performance efficiency and your output quality. Encourage your team members to do the same. It will help you and your team members to keep a focused state of mind if you write down your long term goals and short term goals for the whole team to see. This way, no matter how long and tedious a task may become, you don't get sidetracked on your objectives. You'll be able to propel your workforce back to the right direction no matter how long is the interval between one goal-step to another.

ONE LAST MESSAGE

"We are what we repeatedly do. Excellence, therefore, is not an act but a habit" — Aristotle

If we're honest with ourselves, this quote will resonate within. We are most known by what we do, not what we say. If we are consistent in our actions and our work ethic, people take notice. Success is a measure of doing the common things uncommonly well. Don't do a good job, do a great job!

By following these principles, you should have no issues in increasing to your next level of Leadership and moving your way up in the success ladder. Consistently successful behavior translates to excellence. Truly successful people have integrity, a strong work ethic, a desire to succeed and the tenacity to keep working and to keep learning even when things aren't going well. They don't give up easily; they keep moving forward, regardless of how many times they're knocked back.

I have been through some incredible life events. I have had great success and more than a few failures with my dreams and projects. The principles of Leadership in this book are the lessons that I have learned and adapted in my life to help me succeed. I believe that the true success is not achieving the end result but the journey to achieving that success. What you learn and who you become on the way is the true to success.

Two things I have learned on my way and I believe we can agree on, is that you miss all the shots you don't take and there is no traffic at the top of the freeway to greatness.

Make sure to always be honest with yourself. Work hard. Don't give up. Be consistent and persistent. Do a great job with everything you commit to and enter every commitment with success on your mind.

Don't wait for success to come to you. Be proactive to ensure that you attain the success you desire. Take the initiative to do more than is expected of you each day. Be excellent in your work. Then, when the opportunity presents itself, make the most of it. Ask yourself every day, "Am I consistent in my actions? Do I do my best work each and every day? Am I providing my commitment to excellence rather than mediocrity? Am I doing more than is expected?" If you can answer yes to all those questions, you are truly "Starting With YOU in Leadership".

Remember, don't ever stop investing into your continued education with personal development. You must always continue raising your personal development level so you can continue raising your success level. Never expect your success level to be at a 7 to 8 while your personal development level is at a level of 4 or 5.

I live by a moto and that is to always inspire, motivate and empower others and by doing so I believe that success will manifest within my life. So I encourage that you do the same and that is to pay it forward by passing along a copy to your friends and family so you can help to make a positive difference in their lives and you too can manifest success within your life by blessing others.

Thank you again for reading this book. Make sure to read it a couple more times until these principles become second nature.

Mike Driggers

> "ALWAYS BE A DO IT FIRST LEADER. DO, SHOW, THEN TELL WHY!"

ABOUT THE AUTHOR

Mike Driggers Is a Top selling author, International in demand celebrity speaker, the world's leading Authority Marketing Agent, consultant, business owner and master strategist who inspires, motivates, and empowers people worldwide. Mike has been featured on ABC, NBC, FOX, CBS, PBS, USA Today, Business Journal, Wall Street Journal and the Brian Tracy Show. Mike is recognized as one of the world's most requested business, sales & marketing consultant. He is an in-demand international celebrity business and motivational keynote speaker who has delivered over 2500 presentations worldwide. Mike consistently wows audiences with his entertaining and interactive keynotes, seminars, workshops, coaching, and training programs.

Mike is the author of several books titled "Mastering of The

Mind Set", "Unleash The Intrapreneurship Within", "Nothing in LIFE Starts Until YOU Start", "Nothing in SALES Starts Until YOU Start" and "Nothing in LEADERSHIP Starts Until YOU Start" "Managing Your Commitment". Mike has also co-authored several books titled "Entrepreneurs On Fire" with Barbara Corcoran from the hit TV series, The Shark Tank, "Reach Your Greatness" with James Malinchak from the featured hit ABC TV Show Secret Millionaire", "On Target Marketing" with Vince Baker co-owner of On Target Marketing Group.

Mike has shared the stage with many great thought leaders like James Malinchak, Brain Tracy, Jon Assaraf, Jack Canfield, Zig Ziglar, Jim Rohn, Les Brown, Loral Langemeier, Rudy Ruettiger, Eric Worre, Jeff Olson, Kevin Harrington, Forbes Riley, Glenn Morshower, Seth Godin, Jill Lublin, Kevin Clayson, Richard Kaye, Joel Comm, Darin Adams, Craig Duswalt, Trish Carr, Berny Dohrmann, Shane Gibson, Seth Greene, David Hancock, Sharon Lechter, Nancy Matthews, Ken McArthur, Nick Nanton, Greg S. Reid, E. Brian Rose, and much more.

Mike has been in the top 10% of producers for the direct sales industry for more than 30 years. Mike has owned and operated several successful businesses, including a Bay Area marketing and advertising agency called Unleashed Media where In 2004, he was voted entrepreneur of the year in his local area by President Bush.

Mike uses a no-nonsense, highly focused and disciplined approach to creating real results quickly. He covers subjects including entrepreneurship, mindset, leadership, sales, marketing, high performance, and motivation. Mike's passion, desire, and willingness to be a servant leader has inspired and helped thousands of people achieve greatness within their personal and business lives. As a consultant, Mike's is a behind-the-scenes, go-to sales, marketing and leadership advisor for many businesses. His clientele is a Who's Who in the fields of sports, business, entertainment, and politics. He has helped people from all walks of life create amazing results quickly and hit top ranks within their business and careers. Vist www.BookMikeToday.com

THE IDEAL PROFESSIONAL SPEAKER FOR YOUR NEXT EVENT!

Any organization that wants to develop and grow their business to become "extraordinary" needs to hire Mike for a keynote and /or workshop training!

TO CONTACT OR BOOK MIKE TO SPEAK:

IME Publishing Group

(866) 7BOOKME

(866) 726-6563

www.BookMikeToday.com

Info@SuccessWithMikeDriggers.com

Nothing In LEADERSHIP Starts Until YOU Start

"Share This Book"

Retail 24.95

Special Quantity Discounts

5-20 Books	21.95
21-99 Books	18.95
100-499 Books	15.95
500-999 Books	10.95
1,000 + Books	8.95

To Order Go To www.BookMikeToday.com

INSTANT AUTHORITY

Special **FREE** Bonus Gift For **YOU!**

To help you stand out from the crowd
FREE BONUS RESOURCES for you at;
www.InstantAuthorityNow.com

Get your 3 FREE in-depth training videos sharing how you gain trust from prospective customers. This trust will lead to establishing you as an authority, increase web traffic, boost business sales and attract more referrals. You will also learn how to earn the respect in your industry which can lead to more lucrative partnerships.

www.InstantAuthorityNow.com

www.ingramcontent.com/pod-product-compliance
Lightning Source LLC
Chambersburg PA
CBHW061301110426
42742CB00012BA/2009